NEW &
SELECTED POEMS

NEW &
SELECTED
POEMS

STEPHEN BERG

COPPER CANYON PRESS

The Daughters was originally published by Bobbs-Merrill, Indianapolis, 1971.

Grief was originally published by The Viking Press, New York, 1975.

In It and *With Akhmatova at the Black Gates* are published by the University of Illinois Press, 1981 and 1986.

"Rubber Rats" appeared in *Ploughshares*, and "Shoeshine" in *The Three Penny Review*.

"Unfinished Double Sonnet" first appeared in the *Denver Quarterly*.

Some of the chapters from *Shaving* first appeared in *Tri Quarterly*, the *Kenyon Review* and *The Three Penny Review*.

"Homage to the Afterlife" was first published by Harry Duncan, at The Cummington Press, Omaha, 1991, in an edition of 212 copies.

Publication of this book was supported by grants from the Lannan Foundation, the National Endowment for the Arts, and the Washington State Arts Commission.

Copper Canyon Press is in residence with Centrum at Fort Worden State Park.

Library of Congress Cataloging-in-Publication Data

Berg, Stephen.
    New & selected poems / Stephen Berg.
        p.   cm.
    ISBN 1-55659-044-X : $21.00. — ISBN 1-55659-043-1 (pbk.) : $12.00
    I. Title.   II. Title: New and selected poems.
PS3552.E7N4   1992
811'.54—dc20   91-72065

FOR HARRY DUNCAN

CONTENTS

I

from THE DAUGHTERS

THE DAUGHTERS / 11

THE HOLES / 12

THE SOUL / 13

MILK / 14

PEOPLE TRYING TO LOVE / 15

TO MY FRIENDS / 16

A WIFE TALKS TO HERSELF / 17

OLLIE, ANSWER ME / 18

UNCLE WILL, THE GARDENER / 20

BETWEEN US / 21

MOTHER POLITICAL / 22

ON THE STEPS / 24

WILLIAM CARLOS WILLIAMS READING HIS POEMS / 25

FOR THE GHOST OF LI PO / 26

GOOD / 28

CRUTCHES / 29

DREAMING WITH A FRIEND / 30

TIMES / 31

SISTER ANN / 32

WANTING TO BE HEAVIER / 34

DESNOS READING THE PALMS OF MEN ON
    THEIR WAY TO THE GAS CHAMBERS / 35

from GRIEF

GOOSEBERRIES / 45

HEARTACHE / 46

THE KISS / 47

DON'T FORGET / 48

EATING OUTSIDE / 49

FIRST COLD / 50

AT A FRIEND'S BIRTHDAY PARTY
    IN THE GARDEN AT NIGHT / 51

A DAY / 52

PAGE 256 / 53

FOLLOWING IT / 54

WITH AKHMATOVA AT THE BLACK GATES / 55

SUNDAY AFTERNOON / 57

IT IS / 58

ON THIS SIDE OF THE RIVER / 59

AT THE DOOR / 61

TO THE SAME PLACE / 62

DRIVING OUT AGAIN AT NIGHT / 63

RED WEED / 64

WHAT I WANTED TO SAY / 65

REMEMBERING AND FORGETTING / 66

TO THE BEING WE ARE / 68

"IN DEATH I KNOW WELL ENOUGH ALL
    THINGS END IN EMPTINESS" / 70

DUST / 72

THE ANSWER / 73

WHY ARE WE HERE / 74

from WITH AKHMATOVA
AT THE BLACK GATES

LAST MEETING / 83

1909 / 84

1911 / 85

1914 / 86

ROSES / 87

TWO FRAGMENTS / 88

TWO LITTLE SONGS / 89

1922 / 90

NOTHINGNESS / 91

MEMORY / 92

NEW YEAR'S / 100

THREAD / 101

TASHKENT BLOSSOMS, 1944 / 103

1945 / 104

THIS COLD / 105

YOU / 106

FRAGMENT, 1959 / 108

IN THE EVENING / 109

ALONE / 110

ENDINGS / 112

from IN IT

LEAVES / 117

THE ROCKS / 118

VISITING THE STONE / 120

TO CHARLIE / 121

BOTH / 122

LAST ELEGY / 124

THREE VOICES / 126

THE VISIT / 129

AND THE SCREAM / 130

IN BLUE LIGHT / 132

THE VOICE / 133

SUMMER TWILIGHT / 134

SAD INVECTIVE / 136

ONE / 137

IN WASHINGTON SQUARE / 139

A GOD / 141

NO WORD / 143

SKETCH / 144

OBLIVION / 145

FROM THE BRIDGE / 147

GRATITUDE / 149

IN IT / 151

II

NEW POEMS

CHERRIES / 157

WRITING CLASS / 159

STICKS / 161

PRAYER / 162

LAMENT / 163

RUBBER RATS / 164

SHOESHINE / 165

THROUGH GLASS / 166

BANDAGE / 167

UNFINISHED DOUBLE SONNET / 168

from SHAVING

IOWA / 173

TALKING / 176

THE COAT / 179

BROTHERS / 182

SELF-PORTRAIT AT SIX / 185

BEHIND US / 187

MUSIC / 190

BREAD / 192

LOWELL: SELF-PORTRAIT / 195

NOT THAT / 197

LIGHTBULB / 199

HOMAGE TO THE AFTERLIFE / 203

I

from

THE

DAUGHTERS

The Daughters

Once I knew, nothing in the leaf could see me,
nothing in the word could tell me what it was,
and the daughters sleep with one arm thrown out to the infinite,
their wish for sunlight on waves needs no future,
and the daughters pass through all forms in a single day,
their laughter gives us the ancient joy of the Gods,
and the daughters kiss without vengeance, they kiss,
nothing escapes the blessing of their love, nothing hits back,
and the daughters bring home a twig stone or feather cupped
        in their hands
and save the world with these by pointing to them awed,
and the daughters protect the sacred wisdom of speech,
they say anything with complete faith, and forget it,
and the daughters make war more perfectly than the President,
it begins and ends, it is not waged in secret,
I have read their simple misspelled canticles on a blackboard
amazed as they are at the tininess of a fly's wing, and screamed,
and not known where I was and hugged them and wept –
I want to pray like that, like the daughters always budding,
and the daughters lift food to an enemy's lips if he is hungry,
I see them skip in and out of death without a thought, in ecstasy,
they take and demand and surrender, they go empty –
I wish I knew what love was, I could forgive everything,
and the daughters touch anything and play under the sad wings
of parents, slowly as they grow the dreams begin, less
little and more sprout from their breasts like quills,
the daughters lashed in fire at the gates.

The Holes

Suddenly I remember the holes,
suddenly I think of a man with no entrances,
no exits, the closed man, with feelers or claws
so sensitive that he can tell
what rock is, or flesh, water or flame.
Where does everything go when it comes in?
What should I do with the pure speech of cells
where we find ourselves?
The river flies, the dusk crawls into the ground,
the moon has our face backwards,
the streets get up and leave,
the sun recklessly feeds our blood.
We could be crouching on the branch, we could be
gnawing the brown feathers and thighs of a new animal,
we could be plotting under the ice while others dream.
But I want the infinite man who sleeps
in my veins to rise, I want to hear
the thin buzzing that floats out of my chest
like an arm of locusts making terrible decisions.
Sometimes I want to die because of this.

The Soul

They can tell me the soul rises to its perch,
wing for mouth claw for hand cloud for skin.
They can say "I heard my father's voice last evening
sing like rain poured into a living ear . . . "
They can invent the white book using the black
and beat on the invisible doors beyond behind not here
and push through like the leaves droning.
They can sit with legs crossed in the holy silences
breathing until the universe runs home like a dog,
eternity for Thursday resurrection for Goodbye.
They can put the nakedness of children before war.
They can pray for the suffering whose tongues drown
and apologize and explain and draw me in
whispering "His face holds the star the seed in the brow . . . "
Meanwhile I have heard stones cracking in the eyes
of a teacher, bees entering a lawyer's throat,
the cup's smooth narrow lips trying
to communicate with the housewife's boredom.
Meanwhile the soul prepares entrances for the crow,
exits for the dust, flesh for the heaven of kings.

Milk

Each morning a woman opens the door
and looks
and picks up five bottles of milk.
A faint scraping blurs the air.
Nosebleeds, dizziness, all the signs
of a loneliness nothing can cure,
plague her.
She pours milk for her sons, she
dresses herself and dreams of nothing
in the stuff she pours
and of the great anxiety of
not having enough.
For weeks I have not seen her.
The men drink water.
Who knows what the conversations leave out
or whose mouth churns forever
in silence?

People Trying to Love

step into my room tonight
their hands float ahead of them
their legs open
in answer to the many

For thirty-two years I have lived
and known the black iron
railings of houses
instead of you

Now even that part of me
I will never know knows
I have stayed between my own fingers
too long
believing I did not need you there

It is quiet between our bodies
as we open ourselves
to the one shame
and feel what we lose
the wire stems of poppies

Trying so hard to remain
now even hatred is a false petal
shaking under the rain
sacrificed
to the many

For thirty-two years my hands
have wanted to be other things
cups pliers hammers hooks
wings belonging to a child
they touch you.

To My Friends

Holding its huge life open to the sky,
snow fringes the scaly cones on this hilltop;
I can see it cupped and pierced by the rich needles.
This far from the city, it takes weeks to melt,
and nothing passes on the road that reaches me here
at the back of my house, planted above the river
of headlights. Do you remember that sad movie
where Bogart loses everything and begins
a new life after his plane takes off through the fog,
where he becomes an underground fighter, and poor?
It haunts me tonight because I am not myself
and, wedged between ceilings and floors,
I can feel the tight path of my hands over the keys
get wider. Because those bare, lasting pines
are understandable, because I am here
and not here, because of the silent breath
rising from different lungs,
because these hands are yours, I remember
something no one will ever tell us. Our life,
more like those trees than we are, is the snow;
the stars know it, the dirt road says it again
each time I stop for a minute and listen to the strange
human words of the hedges scraping together, and go in
where the moonlit weedy spaces continue.

A Wife Talks to Herself

A few days ago
my father sent me a box
of wintergreen to replant
so I won't forget him.
I wonder if he saw
the rims of the short notched
leaves get brown
or missed much of the young odor
before he mailed them,
and thought they might look scorched
by the hot passage
from his yard in South Carolina
to this room of mine.
Today, among other things,
I bought soil
and packed it against the roots
of his gift. If that fails,
I'll write him that
there is still nothing more
I can say than this to the message
he gave me through
these wild masks: it is natural
to be shy with one's daughter,
but when I see those curled,
lost faces trying to live
I feel my back stiffen
and remember that once,
passing a stranger
whose thin coat brushed the ground,
I couldn't find
my way home
or recognize myself
in the tiny person
looking at me out of his eyes.

Ollie, Answer Me

When I pictured you
lifting the old people out of bed,
emptying their pans and glasses,
wheeling them down the hall
and reading to them until their eyes
drifted upward like bubbles,
it was impossible to explain
how you got there.
I began by imagining myself
buying everyone daffodils,
sneaking into the fluorescent ward
after curfew to watch them sleep
and listen as they wheezed
and kept you awake.
And even when I created their dreams
about streets that no longer exist,
and yours about cows and a drowsy father,
that was no answer.
Were you a sentinel
called there to report death
and cancel it somehow,
and if you were God's replacement
what can you say about it?

Late one night, visiting you
with friends, I pushed open the door
where you were staying
and a chalk lady
saw someone who looked back at her
and said Hello.
Tell me, did I speak to a face
or to nature? Who was I trying to reach?

I will go on asking you
what we were doing there
and what you learned
because I am everyone who was not there
and could not feel your thin hands
cup his head into the air
for transparent food
or bunch pillows under his neck,
or see you kneel at the side of a bed
barely dented with the weight
of a human body.
And explain this—each night since then
I have heard the stupidity of the words
you sang out of good books
so they would rest and understand.

Uncle Will, the Gardener

Winter had spoiled his Georgia
because the prize roses in the yard
of the lady who paid him
were dying off. Drunk, guided back there
by a ghost of habitual love,
he dropped his dull head to the first dry
petals he could find, and wept.
Frost netted the stem bottoms
in frail multiplications,
threatening the brittle heads.
Standing at the kitchen door, I watched him,
dressed in the old clothes of three
white relatives, and I thought
there is justice in the economy
of nature, although he can't believe
the death of his closest friends.
A gust ripped the heads off some,
leaving their tall dirty stalks naked,
like markers for the bones of the poor,
and, helpless to change, he began
cutting through the cold talkative flowers,
swinging his arms, bringing down all of them
before the next wind could do it.
Later we spoke of the ice
of this world and of the invisible
destruction that takes what men live for.
I agreed with all he said, but I
heard nothing, understood nothing
except the hilly scar on his cheek.
It seemed, through private sorrow,
to smile and be his true mouth,
not mortal, open to its darkest part,
and coiled something like a rose arched out
just before its petals blacken.

Between Us

It is snowing heavily again.
I have been watching it for a long time
the way a blind man looks at the world
on the back of his eyelids.
Something I wanted in my hands
is not there, and I hear
the soft cry of the flakes approaching.
Trapped among branches,
it sounds as if I have lost someone
and have reached up to find
that same whiteness on my mouth,
plunging into itself without me.

Mother Political

Now I need to forget the pages I can't forget and can't read again
where it says men kill men, men are political forever, life,
our life, a leaflet in the third person, floats into the city streets,
are you listening? On which page does it say You know your life
     enough?
on which page can you find Do this, Not that! Free everyone because
you know enough, on which page is the truth wonderful like your
     first word?
Mother of my mother, clay, sky, this is not a poem, this is not
the ninth page of a book, this is not me or you or a river,
this is not the seventieth bullet that tore through Lorca's right
     shoulder
before he fell, this is not the silence of those stark telescopic poems
Teresa scratched into her own skin with fingernails that fought walls
and got nowhere with them, with teeth that chewed iron bars,
you can't read them, you can't tell me she said what she said,
because this is how what is never becomes what will be, this
     is political,
because we're good, we saved everyone, we made mother political,
see her crying when you leave, born for this,
see her laughing in the bathroom to herself when you hit back,
and the bombers are still coming back from Germany, the bombers
still gliding down in Viet Nam, there are still shadows of men
     vaporized
on walls with their mouths open that the light comes through,
their last words exploded so far back into time
eternity was made longer by them, ferns, memory, clouds,
     mother so political,
you so human,
terrified in bed late at night when the darkness attacked, when
the politicians went down on their knees in the fields of
     Granada rye
looking for the bullet, wondering how long a kiss should last, hosing

the jail cell so not one trace of blood of shit of a man's puke
        would be left,
and mother so political, us, just us, sitting around, our tiny bird-
mouths open unfed cheeping Not Enough stuffed with pages
        we can't read—
"they were never there, they were not political, they did not sing,
with this volley two dead Spanish angels killed all the starving
        of the world
in their bedrooms because of a girl"—
written so we could sleep political.

On the Steps

I see
a bunch of old Jews sitting around, mumbling
to themselves in prayer,
but I'm outside waiting.
The synagogue's yellow and blue windows tell
the sun's path as I stand there
listening to what must be a hidden song
to the one God.
These past weeks between winter and spring
I have thought of myself walking in, seeking
the blue flame that rose between the hands
of Hasidic masters as they danced, entering it;
being the Rabbi's wife
who hauled two jugs of wine from the basement
for those dry-throated joy-crazed worshippers
whose hands woke God.
I hear
"There's not enough!" her first words
before she saw them, and the silence
I fear somewhere inside me lifts its tiny
cry to the name,
because how can I eat love know death die and be
          someone's other
unless I'm a poor breath chanted into the air
          through rotted teeth
on the songs of old men?
Well, here I am outside, a man
who can neither share wine nor dance.
Clouds pass, cars pass, people
I haven't seen in twenty-five years speak to me.
Through hard green prongs on a branch, one,
yellow and blown with leukemia, dips his face
to my face.

William Carlos Williams
Reading His Poems

I'm listening to your tired shaky old voice
move in New Jersey over the poems
like ice forming on puddles.
It's sad to hear you sound like that after the strokes,
stumbling, glazed,
after so much raw ball-breaking conversational song.
Spring in Philadelphia, grayish cold, not like
your spring dotted with the blue-eyed flowers
of memory and death, not with a doctor's eye
for the wonder of disease. But there's
snow in April here, like your voice, workers
yelling trustfully at each other, like your voice,
windows trembling in the drone of a huge jet
like your voice nearly cracked by its dedication
to the elements which killed you.
I turn the record off.
In the middle of a poem,
somewhere, either in my mind or yours,
invisible pieces of glass drop to the floor.
I think of Russell's "unbearable pity for the suffering of
        mankind,"
I think of my sixty-one year old father fantasizing young girls
alone at night in his bedroom.
Hearing you this sunless afternoon
was like walking barefoot across some old starry
floor everyone is afraid of and loving it.

For the Ghost of Li Po

Tonight in Philadelphia, I saw you, Li Po,
banished immortal,
a poor man who always had plenty of wine.
Tonight I walked down to the Delaware
in the heat of summer
to see if I could kiss your ghost
swimming in rags
among the white leaves of the moon,
that tree without roots
celebrated by the torn fire of stars
on the water.

When Tu Fu saw your eyes flash in a dream
he saw all of us, drunk, liars,
hating examinations and jobs.
Now you drift like the blade
of the new moon behind the masts of tankers,
tall as the shoulders of your children.

I wish Tung-t'ing Lake was nearby
so you could pass it again
on your way back out of exile,
so I could wait there
to ask you for a gulp of the amber wine of Lu,
so we could scale fish together
and roast them
and eat those "tokens of deep feeling."

I can just see you waking up tomorrow
on the porch of your house,
wobbly as a cricket, singing
and brooding until the moon comes by
and breaks in your cup.

I can see you offering a luminous pill
to the Emperor.

Man with nothing after his name,
you think of soldiers smeared on the bushes
and grass of your village,
you thirst for the purple sash,
you drink your guts out quietly,
weeping, failing, watched by four wives,
your hair a long white wave in the Bay
of The Fallen Star.

Good

It's a little thing,
the word my wife says to me
unexpectedly in the middle of a page I'm studying.
But it opens a door
I can't see, don't want to see,
and I turn both eyes in its direction
where a light swells,
where I thought nobody lived anymore.
Remember that spot on the beach in Margate
where there were no people? well,
one morning while you and the kids were asleep
I went there. Thousands of fiddler
crab shells washed up in a border of foam
just above the water, cigarettes too.
I heard the waves hiss as if I had forgotten
how they sounded, and I thought
it's because the sun fell into the ocean.
It was my daughters running down the beach, screaming
"Daddy!" waves collapsing against the jetty,
the word finding its home in the third body
of my mind. Like whose mouth on my mouth
at the beginning of death?
The light has grown over us and covers us
and, I don't know, maybe we'll never understand
"the foot says
because I am not the hand
the ear says
because I am not the eye"

Crutches

Something in me hates being here.
Something in me cuts and sews until the wound
smiles at the knife and the needle.
Something is a wave under the clear thread
and it breaks endlessly.
Something dissolves and opens.
Something always says "No."
How could I have been blind to it for so long?
I can't strangle it or shoot it.
All I can do is talk, when it lets me.
Then silence rots like snow in my belly.
I wait. I look at everything in my room.
I ask childish questions. I call my friends.
Something in me is nothing until I fill it,
but the other mouths of hell wait for this.
These crutches I rub with the sleeve of an old shirt,
this self, these meat-eating flowers,
hate the second me the way God hates evil.
Something is in me forever. Even after
I sleep it goes on using its helpers,
iodine, rain, stitches, eyelids and milk,
whipping flesh until the merciful cures.
What can I do
when it starts again and plunges its claws
into the slush of my lost body and scoops my heart out
and bites it and expects me to rise?
Something never lets me die unless I die.
Meanwhile I squeeze the edges of my chair
and hear "This is happening! This! This! This!"

Dreaming with a Friend

Your brother is dead.
His breath is one of those lost autumn days
you love.
Your mother works in the kitchen again,
beating eggs.
Ashes drift in from factories,
brush fires
cling to the door.
I see you crossing a field toward me,
not knowing
whom you will find,
kicking weeds.

The dream you told me about is a place
where I touch your head
and you turn.
But I could be anyone.
Your brother sits on the porch again,
crying.
Your mother comes down in the rain.
You see me crossing a field toward you,
not knowing
whom I will find,
following the cracked weeds
turning as you turn

toward someone.

Times

No one is here today, the streets
fill with rain, drops echo in long puddles
near the walls. I'm talking to you again
but you don't hear.
      In my childhood there's a room
where I sit in bed listening to the radio, un-
raveling the edge of a blanket with my lips. The blue
twilight ceiling, heavy and soft as wool, trains
jumbled in a box, a tin
horse galloping forever,
then sleep – I think about this often.
         Like now
without anyone. Tell me what your life is like, call.
Sometimes I dial your number in a rich Jersey town
and can't speak. I know what to say,
         but there are
times when I'm sure I can
cross the street and go up and find you
sprawled on the floor studying, playing records,
smiling because I'm there. There are times,
and we grow distant over the years, and live
somebody's life, ask nothing, and live.

Sister Ann

Come to my room off the street, come into the greasy shadows
of wicker and enamel, into the pierced flaming lips of my mouth,
come out and sit with your hands turned up into my face
over blank linoleum seas, under knickknacks and crosses
and incense curling along paper curtains, come, come
to the impossible infinite eternal perfect great healing
to the powerlady of evil and sickness and bad luck spirits
come to the stink of suffering the fragrance of hope and tin
remover of pain trouble spells death failure ignorance hate
give yourself O man to this lady of the heavenly gift
the trance the lost self the dress bursting with orchids
and the white gypsy blouse the long wobbly breasts the kind
faithful stark eyes of truth come come come to the prayers
of one who has cared is divine come to the Indian of smiles
sit now and listen and see and be given the vision of a self
in the crescent of silence in the black light of the soul
come into the golden smoke the gardenia the velvet the hair oil
where your face drifts like a raincloud or like a wedge of birds
where your hands grow new animal fingers and clutch new things
where you search like dust for a home and are done searching
where the floor swims and the walls come apart and ask you
where the door chants and opens and calls you to fly through
where the window rises like flame like heaven like nothing
now now now now now where she sits like a tumor and listens
where the wise fat of her legs whispers and brings you to
where the daughters of the pig wait where the knives of your bone
where you and you and you and whoever it is have never been
where the bricks begin shifting like words where laughter
where the sty of your cheeks is a desert where stone is the bed
where yesterday shimmers in the rotted fringes between rooms
where the beads clink where the lids pray where the neck shows
where the stockings dance without legs where the toes curl
where the skin falls like a wave where the beach is a good hand
where the sink coughs to itself and leaks into your chest

where the stranger dies with a grin with a straw on his lip
where the naked vein where the talk pours where you change
into where you change where the finger traces the line
where the word and the line are the truth where the nail
where kneelers and askers and failers and hopers and risers
where you find out the miracle of the tongue of red feathers
where everything is you Sister Ann where the crotch is burning
where the green secret numbers flash on the wall and mix
where all my friends have gone have been healed and are saints
where my mother and father have gone not to die and are living
where my children are sent and are better and are glad, still,
where the teachers die and the masters die and the dead die
where the pencil spills its lead like a blizzard over the city
where the bottle of milk turns to an ocean of permanent ink
where the how and why are a furnace of bread and metal
where the poor shine out like gold coins and the rich are weeds
where the tree sings and is fed where the hills are merciful
where the morning creeps like a turtle into my endless laughter
where the crow and the dove breed for the future of men
where no one weeps where no one laughs where no one speaks
where the earth spins like a corpse in the old speckled abyss
where I remember everything the tennis court the arrowheads
the trips the smell of dresses the grades the cheating the sperm
the bicycle the crib the rainy day when he died the bad heart
the vomit the checkers the ass of a naked parent the stolen toys
the beatings the friend burning the insects the light the soap
the new shoes speaking the oracular yes
where anger anger is the name of everyone you love where
        the carrot
and the potato are sprouting on the windowsill
where you are tiny where the dog and the ant and the goldfish
are closest where the sheets turn like ghosts against your desire
where the closet is a box where the toilet is infinite
where the child tumbles forward and has nothing to hold
where it is never tomorrow where the mirror is empty forgotten
where plans are a lie where people are you where you are
where you are always lost where she begins again her predictions
where she does what others call impossible all the way back into

Wanting to Be Heavier

People are chewing on wood.
All those letters about ourselves we mailed to friends
have been collected and sent back and huddle
on doorsteps. All the words have died out.
The blind silent anger that lifted pens
and dragged them across paper is all that's left.
This is what happens when the parents wake up.
This is the revolt of the ghost fathers
who got less love than they needed from their sons.
This is how wives live forever after the marriage battles.

Now there's nothing for me but the last saint's hair, flaring
like a star, nothing except distance and prayer.
Now those who listened are trying to write back.
They drift into my eyes as the sweet clouds from bakeries,
they choke me with the sour breath of cars,
they have signs plastered on walls that the rain licks.
Wanting to be heavier, I do bad things.
I build statues of my mother with putty and salt.
I talk only if the wind rattles a flag or sings through a keyhole.
I gnaw pencils and print my name.

Desnos Reading the Palms of Men on Their Way to the Gas Chambers

Our suffering would be unbearable if we couldn't
think of it as a passing and sentimental disorder.

—ROBERT DESNOS
March 28, 1944, Buchenwald★

Maybe I should go back to the white leather
sofa and bull terrier
of my childhood, when my grandfather died,
but I can't.
It rained and there were beaks of light.
Who was it
picking my hand up where it hung
against my naked thigh?
What matters is how we act before we die,
whether we have a joke ready
and can make all the terrified sad faces
around us laugh and weep,
whether we can make everyone kiss.
Who was it? Who holds us here?
Whom should we touch?

You squeeze my hand.
The orchestra's notes from across the road
weave upward in the smoke,
the frozen eyes, the brown angular light
off center, rows, stacks, glasses
without anyone's eyes behind them
and nothing except
the smile of a boot,

★ It is reported that the French poet, Robert Desnos, broke out of a line
of naked prisoners on their way to the gas chambers at Buchenwald and
went from prisoner to prisoner reading palms, predicting good fortune
and happiness.

35

the eyes of gloves,
the mouth of a belt
and the holes.
Holes.
I squeeze your hand.

You don't love anyone.
I'm sorry. You never loved anyone.
Probably it's because your planets
are mixed, or Jewish.
But there's a cross down by the wrist
on the edge of the mound of Venus
and lines tangling violently
along the third finger.
You're a sexual person.
Still, those lines webbed
under the thumb are bright.
The agony is false.
The earth has been here beneath us
less than an hour
and we are shuffling forward.
Nobody looks at us.
Say anything,
say we are somewhere else,
each violin has
long curved eyes
tilted seaward and up
like your hand in mine.

And yours, little boy with dark brown eyes,
is wetter than the fake soup
of urine and grass the Nazis give us.
You hide your penis fearfully
behind it, making a pathetic cup
while the other hand dangles
like a noose
that will open on no one,
close on no one.

But I predict one last moment of
incredible joy
when you see yourself melt
into the hundreds gasping around you,
and the doors are pulled
and the gas sighs once, reminding
the Father of you.

Nothing is lost. One guard sprouts wings
in his sleep. He is presented a robe of
spun blond hair and a throne
of tiny nuggets.
In the morning on the parade ground
he opens his fly and prays for us
and is shot
and chopped up for the dogs.
But the next night he returns,
an amputated wing
branding its shadow in miniature
on twelve foreheads.

Like a blind clown I dance between
rifles and the laughter of kings,
and it must be my withered cock and balls,
the color of stone walls,
that cause so much happiness
in the ranks,
as I stumble through the prisoners to hold them,
needing to touch as many as I can
before I go.

There's a shallow hole over the bed
on the wall behind my head
where my dreams live on
after I have waked and knelt
and bled
thousands of times.
I look into it and if I concentrate

I see bodies decorated with
God's toil and ashes.
They drift
into the mouths and eyes
of the living
until there is nothing
but children
like us
here.

Shaggy grains of frost
cling to the ground.
The barracks glitter, the sky hugs
itself like a girl whose arms
have been hacked off, and the wire
hums invisibly in the night air except when a
strand goes white for a second
from no source.
O I want to be that thread, tiny
barrier, bodiless vein, line
that the wind reads.
When I chew on what looks like a finger
and tastes like sour wine
I remember you running, stretching your arms out
to be caught or to fling yourself
through space
until your laughter choked in the sand.
I remember nothing.

You ask me why.
I stand facing you
and speak your name,
whatever it is.
Your name over and over
like a lullaby
until we kiss.
I put my hand on your breast.

It is beautiful, and ugly,
and as empty
as we will be soon.
Lights begin passing
in your eyes
like cities going to sleep
or like those thick lamps on the masts
of fishing boats.
I love you more than I
have loved anyone.
You touch my hair and cry.

Are you different from the one
I just touched? Who are you?
Everyone looks so young suddenly
as if this were the beginning
of the world.
Everything is as silent as this hand
laid up in my palm,
except for a slight hissing somewhere.
What would you say if I spoke?
I will marry a beautiful woman
named Youki,
have children, a cottage
in the forest near Compiègne
and live many years?
I will marry and have children.

Sometimes a message flutters down,
and someone picks it up
and reads:

then goes back home.
The wheels clack.

Unbearable, the wrong parents, the sun
funneling down like the wings

of judgment. Love suffers.
                              I
dance in any direction now,
kissing the guards, soothing their faces
with my torn hands, singing like a child
after a long illness
who is here, here and here,
knowing you by the lost warmth
of your hands
in Philadelphia, Cape May,
New York, wherever I could not be.
Who is it?
I slide under the uniforms
and fill them,
and as I swim the sorrow and depth
of a stranger's blood, of
a belly held in by a bulletproof vest,
I know it was not a mistake
to be here.

I am my sister, but I have none.
My brother, but I have none.

Living men, what have you done?
In a strand
of invisible scorched nerve
scenes we won't remember
never stop flashing toward us,
unreceived,
like us.
The last wisps of gas
rise from our sleeves

and what I danced is danced again where
you smile about love
and eat with friends
the last smile is smiled first

and I am both of them
on the last mouth

and I am the light you see by
fingers tracing the breast
a cloud chilling the street suddenly
what you need, say, lie down
next to in hours
of common terror
I am the face
touch touch

and who it is is who it is

a boot's O empties itself eternally
as radiant in the holiness
of presence as
any

I go back
and can't
but I hear myself
call the flesh
call what I love
what I love is not listening

Don't you hear it?
It says "The pain will soon be over"
It says "The lovely season is near"

Don't you hear it?

from

GRIEF

Gooseberries

I can't sleep tonight, can you?
It is the voice of Gooseberries whispering
we are not good enough to be happy.
Near sleep, when your face gazes at itself
through a window or against a pale floor,
I hear you scratching on the wall of my room.
Forget about happiness. Tomorrow, when we
meet outside on the steps of our houses,
show me how to kiss your sad lips, tell me
what I can give you.
The fat owner who is happy is not you,
eating jam near the glue factory, drinking
tea, bathing in the river,
his wet hands lifted to the dying sun.
In a dish the gooseberries do not wait
and the doctor who did not believe in God
still asks forgiveness, and he is you.
I can smell the clean sheets where Burkin lay down,
suspicious of burnt tobacco.
He thought the stink came from something else.
It was hours before he could sleep and touch you.
Rain beat against the windowpanes all night.

Heartache

AFTER READING THE CHEKHOV STORY

The horse is breathing on his hands.
The night sky fills his mouth.
It takes many words to say that his son is dead
and many nights to finish,
but the animal is patient. Even the limp flakes
blowing between their heads are a listener,
and riders with troubles of their own,
drunk and in pain and feverish,
are dreaming about a boy they have never met.
Some watch helplessly while he calls and drowns.
Some push a knife into a stranger's neck.
Some twist like keys in a lock on the wrong door.
Some have all the time in the world and a wall of snow.
Some still concentrate on hooves kindling the black street.
Well, the tears of an old man are not important,
especially tonight. Sleep is the one we love.
But a grief in rags leans up to a thick dirty ear
and speaks and his breath melts a hole in the air
and the years break like infinite mornings on the faces,
white, imperceptibly shrinking, of men asleep
that would not listen.
The rows of stark yellow teeth grinding a slow liquid,
the rasp of a man's throat explaining without words,
the jangle of passengers' keys in a pocket,
what seem like answers in the jolts of a huge head—
continue. Drifts climb under the lamps.

The Kiss

AFTER READING THE CHEKHOV STORY

I put my book down and open it
and say "page 53."
Lying on each other like dried skins,
the pages whisper,
my head fills with the sting of
peppermint from a girl's tongue.
The edges of the sky turn gray.
We are leaning next to each other
in old steel chairs, we are gray.
Shadows tremble in a corner.
The words on the paper, like our breaths,
belong to the lost altars of blood,
to a soldier's mouth.
Someone swallows, someone begins to cry.
Ordinary people, ordinary lives.

I have taught this story for days,
my hands leaving the desk to explain something
and offer it as a vision, my fists
motionless on the wood. This anger of
understanding is an empty thing, this
hatred of words because they say something
is a useless bridge between us
when we could kiss.
What have we given or taken, and not touched?
The windows have grown colder.
Classes, leaves, clouds are tearing away.
And now I need strange things to happen —
red moon chewing on itself in a bottomless mirror,
river foaming under a cabin,
"How stupid! How stupid!" filling a Captain's head.

Don't Forget

I was always called in early for dinner.
It was dusk usually, half an inning to go,
I'd hear my mother tell me to beat the dark,
everyone would mumble, I'd throw my glove down and leave.

At home, sitting at the table, I'd imagine the score,
and the speckled homework book seemed to watch me
until I opened it, stared at the numbers, and fell asleep.
Damp laundry rustled in the yards of the houses.

Everyone was punished like this because
our parents worried we'd fall, or missed us,
but we always got hurt anyway or would sit for hours
sanding the wings of an enemy fighter plane until they shined

like metal. We climbed walls until we slipped and our legs broke,
our first kisses were so murderous we almost fainted.
Don't forget, this is inside us every day.
We want everything, our hands stop too soon,

and who are we when a face speaks and opens to us
like a wave? The tame grasses of the head, the moist spiral ear,
long water nobody has crossed – you feel yourself leaving,
you can't lift your hands, you stand there, leaving.

Eating Outside

Fat pine boughs
droop over the vegetable garden's
sticks and leaves,
the moon's hazy face comes and goes
in the heat.
Beautiful women,
your skin can barely be seen.
The moon's gone. Clouds everywhere.
A pale hand curls
on the tabletop next to mine,
there's talk about work and love.
We're like the moon at this hour
as clouds swallow it or dissolve so
it glides through the shaggy limbs,
full, like the grief inside us,
then floats off by itself
beyond the last tips of the needles.
The trees are quiet. In the house
my daughters play the piano and laugh.
The family dog races in and out howling.
The candles on the table have blown out.
I keep trying to explain
but when I go back, like now, there's
the red hammock, the barbecue guarding
the lit back wall like a dwarf,
the self, awed by changes,
motioning to us as it leaves.
Deep among those arms, it pauses
clear, white and unseen.

First Cold

There's a raw blue haze
in the branches, cries
of the shrunken world
blow through.
It's dark early, I
see her hands
button my coat at the neck.
I want to be touched in this weather
but why, what do I miss?
The stars are closer tonight,
the trees give their stiff colorless webs
to the sky, the clouds grow
pink, leaves scrape at the walls.
Listen.
A woman sobs. I
tell myself stand here while the leaves curl and scatter.
A red moon tilts its face
to my hands
and seems to answer.

At a Friend's Birthday Party
in the Garden at Night

What creeps in is the awareness of death
just when you're eating dinner, just when you've touched
the sweet thick hair of one of your children
and smell something so innocent of death
in the roots your throat narrows, you have
to say something but what comes out is
a gurgle or nothing. You remember
jumping around in the ocean when *blam*
a wave hits the back of your head and sucks
you under as it curls over you
and you crawl out behind it, your belly
scraped by the sand, your mouth filled with sour water;
you stand up and walk and look for your family
on the beach and can't see them. Then you do.

No accidents, Freud says, but I'm not sure.
Some things convince me accidents exist
like a truth or a feeling that changes my dumb soul,
that can't be called anything, that lives me.
Back to the personal – veins darken the skin
of the thighs of the woman you love, your mother
refuses to speak with you, you lift weights,
think about your diet, meditate on God –
yesterday we drove away from the city.
The trees increased, and the sky and grass,
people stood quietly on their lawns looking happy
and we sat drinking and eating behind the small house,
the light drained from our faces until we could barely see,
and death rode by as itself, I'm telling you,
a fat red cloud all of us yelled at and pointed to.

A Day

The oaks rooted in stone
don't tremble on this windless, February
day. Somewhere upstate it snows, crowning
the shy weeds and wrinkled hillsides.
It will snow here too,
the numb branches
that have no leaves will bend.
I studied their brown skins today,
today I
watched a girl burst into tears
in the middle of a class.
                The day wears on
quietly except for one
vein that throbs when I see
her face explode.
             Whatever
is touched stays what it is
and so do we. Light swells
at the edges of buildings as if it will clear.
But I tell you this voice is almost not here
to speak
because nothing
explains or helps or knows what
we are.

Page 256

When I tell you to read page 256
it's because the story of the occupation
of a small country is told there. First they
dragged each woman under twenty into the street
and made horses fuck them, then the town men
had their balls torn off and thrown into a barrel.
Children were forced to set fire to it.
Page 256 is important
because of its bare, historic detail, its tone of rage,
which the facts muffle.
There were lawns of roses there, and streams
so clear you could comb your hair in them,
stores hung with kitchen utensils,
stalls bursting with fruit. Page 256
is important because ethics is the mystery
of the sexual, together they create justice.
Page 257 contains a photograph
of a family standing on the edge of a door-shaped pit.
Their hands are not raised, they don't look unhappy.
On 258 you'll find an analysis of the religious
need in man and a strange passage that explodes
in one sentence and could be the caption
under the photograph I described –
"History is the miracle of a child's face!"
The unknown author of this book can't understand
what we have done to each other,
can't explain facts, can't keep himself
from stating, whenever he has to –
"We struggle with dream figures but our blows fall on living faces."

Following It

A full moon glazes the city,
its face closer than I've ever seen it, huge.
Clouds hide the bottom of it, blow off,
leaves flood the pavements –
so much of me as I walk home
part of the cloudy moon and the clear moon.

It's like one of those miraculous sweet days from childhood
when I'd wake happy, dress, eat, run out to play
and in a few minutes, it seemed, twilight would come.
I'd sit on the front steps after dinner, my throat brimming
under the sallow lamps, a cool mist dampening everything.

A breeze lifts and sinks over the houses.
There's peace in being alive, full, mysterious.
I remember wishing the moon could see me.
I thought, it's easy being a man, necessary.
I stand on the fire escape, listening.

A siren widens and fades. Breaths
drift up out of the darkness, carrying words.
A cough. Impossible to tell who it is.
One by one they are waking. Harder to find the moon.
The roofs, one roof over us now, glisten.
Faces underneath. Nobody to see them.

With Akhmatova at the Black Gates

I didn't know it would be like this – snow
in the low twenties powdering the sidewalks,
gray and windy like it was at Christmas,
and there's a secret I can't tell anyone, not even myself.

Trees slap their thin hands on the windows,
a record plays, the sun goes in and out,
my life's somewhere between what it was and what it will be
this Saturday morning reading you.

On the book, two photographs of you, young and old,
your suspicious hurt face fogged with sorrow.
I skim the pages and eat and look out
at the scrawny branches until they blur,

I shave and stare into the mirror
as if I don't recognize myself, my eyes caged and vacant
like a girl's I was afraid of twenty years ago, like my father's.
The sink's ice against my groin

and as I dress I know Akhmatova's deep shyness
with men, her thirst to be touched,
the intimacy politics almost killed,
her talk about madness and Russia, overwhelmed her

while the jails crushed her people and her son.
It's a slow, anxious day in Philadelphia, lonely.
I keep seeing your eyes, I want to explain why sleep
in your poetry means you're not alone. It means

"I knew you were dreaming of me, that's why
I couldn't get to sleep." My wife and daughters
work in the kitchen, somewhere the secret white

stone of happiness and suffering, your dead husband,
lies at the bottom of a well, and you're cut off
from everyone in a glittering resort town the rich ski through,
    writing,
cooking, screaming, and "I can't and don't want to fight it,"
    you say,
"only the stone age wind beats on the black gates."

Sunday Afternoon

A gray sky smudges the tops of buildings.
At a children's concert my father looks
into my daughter's face and cries.
My wife's eyes lower. Not a word.
It is Sunday afternoon, nothing to do,
nothing, no meaning to atone for.
Something heavy clings to the air.
The temples are closed.
The small noises of life grow louder.
We are planning to meet each other and kiss.
We expect the salvation of terror to purify us.
Some god, brushing a cheek, an arm, lips,
tracing his absence in our flesh,
feels no shame.
If an angel comes, it will be naked
for the first time, crippled, shining,
calling through the sour haze to us.
Not one more song of light is possible.
One word and the losses will be destroyed.
Don't turn back.
Voice without wings,
the silence that floats down before you get here
is a crown on each man's head.

It Is

The sky's blue and clear usually,
one white star quivers at the top of the bedroom window.
We lie here nights, looking at it,
amazed by existence. Millie says
it's wonderful to see it burning there,
to lie close to each other in bed and just watch it.
She slips a leg under mine, rubs her foot against mine,
sighs, before sleep. I can see a flake of that wild bright
steadiness through her eye when I look over, and it stays there.
When Plato says
we fear death because we think life's important
he means we should see ourselves
in the star, now.
Morning. I dress and wash. The trees
don't have any leaves. Sparrows hop among the branches,
seeking a crumb, discovering our feeder stocked with seed.
Crick crick crick comes from the porch where I hung it.
When they feel me spying on them they spurt away,
their brief persistent cries all around me,
coming from the trees, coming from the air, coming
from the wires and cornices where they sit.
                                        Look.
It begins to rain. Drops grow on the small branches,
slip off, grow back, slip off again,
a stuttering on the roofs and panes.
                              What struggles,
what we call ours, noise like voices from high
or low in the house, something so deep in us
it is us takes over.

On This Side of the River

TO MILLIE

Simply trust:
don't the petals also flutter down
just like that?

—ISSA

I undress and lie down next to you in bed
and throw one of my legs across yours, I wait
until you are completely lost
then slide my head on the pillow with yours.
Your hair gets caught in my teeth.
I stretch a little to rub my head against yours, so
gently neither of us can feel it,
my breath goes and returns with yours.
There is a moon. Clouds streak its face.
At this late hour by the river the cherry trees stand alone,
black tongueless sentinels
that report nothing.
Wind shakes the flowers that hang over the water,
on the other side families sit down to eat.
I know it.
Not one petal has been torn loose,
and I lie here with my hands on you, not moving,
seeing us today under the trees
sitting with our legs crossed facing each other, talking,
and try to remember what we said.
Get up. I want you to explain
what no couple has ever understood—
the silence, our two skins, the fact that one dies first.
One angry face the color of the
blossoms flashes up and leaves.
The moon pours in. I begin telling you about
my life like the cabdriver in the story

who plows all night through Moscow desperate
for someone to listen to him and winds up at dawn
standing under a streetlamp, snow chilling his mouth,
telling his horse how terrible life is because his
five-year-old son died yesterday, and not one passenger
        would listen,
pulling the nag's ear down to his mouth, whispering deep
into it his unbearable story.

At The Door

Black trees. The banks fill with shadow.
Where the roadlamps throw their blue light
on the water, it's alive.
We drive by without speaking.
Everything is so peaceful outside,
and inside, that the deep endless laugh
of a man who has found happiness begins
and I remember my daughters coming up to me
and smiling, saying whatever they wanted to
without fear.
This is enough. Give everything else
to the hungry.
They say each person has a story
but that isn't true.
We live.
The leaves are so dark tonight I can't see them
but I feel them breathe,
the river's moving on but all I see
is wrinkled patches of blue light, squirming.
My father's dying.
He's asleep next to my mother as the car plows
        through.
She sits and waits.
I stick my arm out the window
and let it be a wing.
I know what to do.

To The Same Place

The first warm summer afternoon I ask a friend
to ride out with his two daughters and me.
We park by the river.
Everybody's there, cooking, dozing, biking,
playing ball. We get out and look for shade
and sit under a huge cherry tree.
I envy the steady unpredictable growth
that has taken everything and survived,
I pick at the shiny lumps that have burst through
the papery brownish pink bark. It glows.
Then, knowing there's no escape from grief,
I pick up the whiffle ball and we catch –
curves, knucklers, floaters, anything we can
get going on the calm air and slowly again
the peace I felt
when we drove past this place nights ago
spreads through me.
Now his children crawl over the low branches, screaming,
they jump down and scoop handfuls of parched dirt
and carry it to us.
                    How much is left?
The dusty grains flare between their fingers
and Jeff points out how small the young cherries are
this early, not ready to eat,
and squeezes one
until it pops and its juice stains his fingers.
The branch snaps back.
The children want to eat them.
That's how it is, wanting to eat green cherries,
getting sick. But fathers protect us,
we think, until they die.
Then we stand on the earth
in front of our children, fathers ourselves,
and the bitter taste of love sings on our tongues.

Driving Out Again At Night

A full moon tilts over the lawns and trees.
Pale shadows, pockets of heat,
couples humped along the riverbanks,
these and the invisible road cure me.
The arc lights are out for miles.
I still carry you inside me, Dad, one hundred
and thirteen extra pounds, gray-faced and weak,
but out here the smell
of water and leaves fills me and pushes you out.
I'm sorry. I love you. But I have to let you go.
So we drive away again
into a few blurred things,
my friend and I,
most of the time not talking.
When cars rush by us they blind me
and I like not seeing. We turn left
over the bridge to come back
and a couple dances across the road, caught
in our beams, the boy raises a brown paper
bag with a bottle in it.
Its mouth flashes.
On my left the river is as clear as a baby's eyes.
When I look off toward the stretches of grass, soaked
        in darkness,
sweeping by, I see myself twenty years ago
lying there with a girl
and pound the dashboard with my fist.
Back in the city
the lights on floor after floor of offices stay on.
Nobody's there. The last
shoppers pause at the frozen bodies, glowing
in store windows, then straggle home.

Red Weed

next to me on the riverbank,
I pluck you out of the dirt,
I hold you
between two fingers
because I'm alone.
I wish I could speak through the invisible
roots I have,
not through my face.
You don't have a face,
brown roots going nowhere,
bloody spiked crown.
When I toss you
you sail a few inches
then fall onto the water
and drift away.
There's my father the morning I woke
and saw him. I see him
in me, eyes
open, mouth open,
drifting away.
He didn't wake.
The spot of blood he coughed up on the pillow's
you, red weed,
so tiny, so clear when I held you
up against the sky, so
wise not to answer, god
of the box of ashes,
father.

What I Wanted to Say

I woke at six. Birds cried from the roofs.
No sun yet, a bleak sky and clouds,
the first cars taking men to work. I slept
downstairs on the couch, half the night
I saw your emptied face, your weak shiny hands
that had lost their warmth after the heart attack.
Like water. You could barely talk. I thought
about what we say to each other even now,
and about the white fires of the crematory
furnace that made you ashes.
All this came up as easily as the wind
shakes the leaves on one of the trees outside my house
then stops, and the leaves hang there, so quiet
you believe something miraculous will happen.
The streetlamps glow with a sudden brightness,
you feel satisfied with the cracked chimneys,
the dull orange haze blowing across the stars,
you could sit endlessly on the steps, smoking,
doing nothing, and never speak again.
But this isn't what I wanted to say.
The birds were calling me, I think. Or someone.
There were tears. I stumbled. My jaws ached.
I bent over my sleeping children to say goodbye
and each one turned to me and smiled. But this
came back – your dead face was a blank white
flower opening in me, which I couldn't touch.
I stood somewhere, saying, "Nobody can say this."

Remembering and Forgetting

I don't know where my father's ashes should lie.
I drive to the cemetery
to find out
and when I get there,
passing under the gnarled walnut trees
by the churchlike crematory fortress, on the office
windowsill there's a box the size
you'd wrap a wineglass in for a gift
with brown paper and string around it
and a white label on top,
Sidney H. Berg
typed on it.

I put my
hands around it, around *him*,
and stand there holding it out in
front of me, staring across the field
of thin stones to the edges of the grass
where the streets and houses begin,
like yesterday
at the supermarket when an old man pushed his cart by
and we smiled
and suddenly
I was studying
the long shelves of bread,
crying, lost.

I look through
the maps of possible graves, telling
the director
what kind of place I want my father in.
Maybe a few bushes and trees around it,
I say, and I think of myself

as bushes and trees.
We step out into the cold to
look for a spot but they're all
friendless, naked to the naked sky,
until I see one next to a row of family stones
fringed by purple bushes
on one side under a few young elms.

All this came back
when that old man went by me shopping and
I heard my mother wailing
her loneliness and rage.
Three black men dug the plot
and placed the ashes, I was told.
I wasn't there. I taught classes.
A windy October day,
the sky a blue cloudless glare.
I hope they lowered him gently
the way they would have if I had been there.
Recently, five months since then,
I asked a sculptor I know if she'd pick out a stone
and carve it into a marker and I'm
still

remembering and forgetting to remind her to do it.

To The Being We Are

Nobody's
with me this time.
Gray sky smeared over the gray trees and water.
Nothing's in it.
Each word the sages use to describe God
disgusts me.
Who cares what exists?
Driving. The river on my left.
Long floors of shale cling to the hillsides,
yellow weeds jut right out of the stone,
cars, the road, distance,
they don't stop anywhere.
I'm not here so I see everything,
listen and see,
hands perched on the black shiny wheel
so lightly it steers by itself.
I park and step out on one of the dirt paths
leading to the water and stretch out
by the side of the river and stare into the
cloudless sky until
that's all there is. Not even
my heart. I can't feel anything
except the vast moist breath of the unnamable thing
we live in, someone's mouth close to my skin . . .
forget it.
I know the spirit doesn't exist.
What dies is hatred, and love, too.
And you can call anything anything then.
Today the river didn't move, or the leaves,
or anything except us, bodies tossed anywhere,
held anywhere. Listen. I was trying to
see God, touch God. I laid my cheek on the grass.

I could hear that nation I will be joining under me
celebrating itself, at peace with itself,
chewing things.
I stuck my fingertips into the gritty mouth
of the earth.
I pissed in the bushes.

"In Death I Know Well Enough
All Things End in Emptiness"

I feel wonderful today after a long night
being naked with my wife.
For weeks we hated each other, refusing to speak or touch,
but last night when I got home from work
there was nothing,
nothing except the face of my dead father,
his eyes half open not seeing in or out.
I read the letters you wrote me when he was dying
and wept. You said that what we talked about
when I'd phone you before he died made you remember
how you're afraid sometimes of not finding anybody to help you
when you need it, of how we live trapped between the
        "clayey walls
of life," reaching up for a hand.
I hear the ocean hissing
under his window the morning he died
and my mother screaming down the halls after she found him,
couldn't wake him, then called me.
All those long weeks he was failing I'd call you
and you listened, so delicately aware of my pain that
it was your pain.
              I feel death's leaning
just outside ready to smash in the door and begin on me.
Life cuts me open, but I do what I want to, mostly.
Last night I came home angry and tired and told my wife to love me.
We stared at each other. Soon we touched.
Then we talked about anything
until we knew each other so deeply we took off our clothes and felt
everywhere and clung to each other and fucked
then lay touching until we slept.

Death does this with people.
Her face, his, yours, swim out of the darkness
that terrifies us. We can live.
Three pale blue lights burn in the building
across the street, a few lumps of snow
melt on the sill. My head floats on the pane the way it'll look
years from now, half here, half there, nobody I know
watching the world through it, day
and night gone into each other.

Dust

One last night under a pink sky
I sit near the river's edge alone.
Moths wobble through the grass,
wind is in the leaves and on the river,
threatening rain. That's the smell I love best,
it blew down out of the sky into the drizzly afternoons
of my childhood, promising everything.
Late summer,
the first dry leaves blowing,
father, mother and son
fish over the edge, the old woman's
fuzzy white hair glows in the white moonlight
as she whips her line back past her head and the weight
swings it around until it hisses and sails out and plops
into the broken water.
A rower pulls by, I listen
to the oars
talk to me.
Crickets drone their prayer,
not to anyone or anything in particular.
Arc lights throb on the water. Nobody.
I don't care,
I could sleep out here without any of us
where the sharp horns of the young orange moon point
at the city. Gone.
No meaning, everything at peace.
Even his face, blanker
than the unlighted scowl of the moon,
less than dust.

The Answer

Yes. Autumn. The leaves yellow and red.
When I got up this morning
no clouds, no thoughts, only the sky.
I slept downstairs, redreaming
the dream
where I'm talking with my father
who says he'll meet me for lunch,
his face so undeniably his that when I wake
I'm sure it's real. That's why
I drove out here again. Not that he's here.
I just wanted to be by myself
with the drifting water and bright sky
so I drove fast to the spot I love between
the first stone balcony with its war heroes
and the bronze rower shipping his oars
and slid out and ran under the yellow and red trees
looking up at them as I passed and they passed.
And forgot him.
Because I can now, because
his sad, square, bitterly joking face
rises by itself through me –
the way a cloud floats in suddenly, shifts, breaks up and disappears –
and will until I go
back to the placelessness before us, after us.
It isn't even love that does this, or needing somebody, it isn't
even the sick miracle of being human or the leaves
blown down crackling underfoot.
I can't explain. And I'm happy not trying to.
Today your silence was what I hear every time
I go out at night
and stand still and don't look –
a chanting of stars and ants, the dry
grass and leaves congregating by accident, the buzz
of the empty world, answering.

Why Are We Here?

I'm half awake
and the phone rings,
it's Jeff's wife
asking me if
I know where he is,
one of his patients
needs him to go
to a funeral with her, her
boyfriend was killed last night
in a car accident.
I think for a minute, sigh,

and say I don't know, I go
downstairs to make coffee,
open a book of stories
and begin to read.
It's about soldiers
put out to sea by the government
so nobody will see them die, but I
think about money, a lot of it,
I want to buy
everything with it.
On the first page three men are dreaming.

I feel the futility they feel
in the trance of silence at life's end,
in the fantasy of a fish ripping a hole in the hull
at the beginning of the story,
so I keep reading about them
waiting in the middle of nowhere.
On deck or in sick bay
they talk about how
Christians know nothing, about

fish as big as mountains,
about the wind breaking loose
over the earth like dogs that had been
chained to huge stones
at the end of the world, and they
dream – a pool crusted with snow,
clouds of black smoke
roaring out of a chimney,
a bull without eyes, a brother, a son.
"All that's needed in the first place
is to have no conscience or humanity.
We're only cattle," one says,
and Gusev listens.

These were men once,
torn from their homes to rot.
They want to be gentle
because life doesn't come back,
one praises God, one curses the army,
they go over plans, clean boots, they
hear sleighs hiss through their dreams
where a woman opens
her fur coat
and lifts her foot
to show everyone her new felt boots.

In the middle of a card game
one of them confuses the score,
lets the cards
trickle out of his hands,
smiles, slides to the floor,
and dies.
And one gives a speech –
"Life is protest!"
Another stares out the porthole
at a weird boat swaying
in the bright sunlight

and sees naked Chinamen on it hold up
cages, a canary in each one,
and hears them shout, "It sings! It sings!"
Then it's dark again.
Two days pass.
"God, it would be wonderful
to be home, to hear
the horses wheeze and the runners
whine on the snow and be
turned over and flipped out of
a sled into the snow. . . . "

The heat is stifling. The ship churns through the water.
Gusev and his friend
go up on deck under a clear sky and agree – it's better
when you die at home because
your mother's there to weep over you.
They smell dung and hay, see
oxen tied to the rail. Moonlight
flakes on the water. It's like their villages.
One stretches out his hand and a pony snarls,
bares its teeth and lunges at his sleeve,

and Gusev says, "There's
nothing to be afraid of, only
it's strange like when you sit down
in a dark forest . . . "
Later in bed he wants everything,
he doesn't know what he wants,
he dreams they are just taking
bread out of the oven
in the barracks and he
climbs into it
and takes a steam bath,

lashing himself with birch twigs,
then sleeps for two days and dies.
The last part of the story
is about
what happens to him underwater
after he's been wrapped
in sailcloth and sinks to the bottom.
First pilot fish, frightened
by the dark body, swim away,
but they come back, and a shark
lays its jaws on the body,

taps it with his teeth, then
rips open the cloth
along the whole length of it
and a lead weight slips out.
The sky bulges with clouds
massing themselves against the sunset.
One looks like a lion, one
like a monumental arch, a third
like scissors,
and a giant blade of green light
shoots out,

pierces the clouds and reaches
to the center of the sky.
Soon there's a
purple one beside it,
then gold, then one stained rose,
and "the heavens turned lilac, very soft."
Gazing up at this great sight,
the sea fumes darkly at first
but as I read takes on
those joyous, passionate colors
nobody can name.

I close the book in anger.
Sun floods the doctor-writer's name, its letters blaze
on the bent, smudged cover.
Here's why I started writing this —
I wanted it to be what happens
with people when they
face each other, afraid to touch,
then reach out and touch only when they're
about to leave,
like last night — we
drifted in bed for hours, not speaking, inches apart,

suddenly we slid closer
and played with each other
gently until we made love almost asleep.
Time chills us until we don't know anything.
I see it even in the eyes of strangers
some days, a thing
that feels like it'll explode,
and saw it nest in my father's eyes.
He looked so small I was his father
and could lift him easily
and rock him like a baby.

His face grows inside me.
I stare into it and it
looks back at me, old,
withering and speechless, in bed,
stricken with morphine.
My daughters stare down at me,
my wife stands behind them, crying.
There's a watercolor on the wall — gulls
weave over the ocean, pink and green clouds.
A bottle drips into my arm
but I'm standing over my father, trying

to keep him alive, telling him
I'm writing, the kids are fine, bringing him
magazines and Kleenex.
He groans the Mafia's taking over
his hotel in Florida, he says the nurse is a stewardess
on the plane. When I leave him, with a kiss,
and walk down the baby-blue, disinfected corridor
I put my head on my fists
against the elevator door and see us
leaning on each other when I was five
in a scorched field, his left hand curled on my shoulder.

Yesterday Jeff told me
he's going to call in the whole family
of the girl whose boyfriend died
and find out why they don't love.
Why are we here? In this story
of theirs, of his, of ours,
pain's everywhere,
we appear as others and as ourselves.
But how? Yesterday
I drove everyone
to the University Museum

and saw water lilies
at rest on the surface of a pool.
Their leaves were
flat, tilted like fans held up, or curled,
as if they were asleep or about to take off or
hesitantly pointed to the blank sky.
That's how we are, I thought,
watching them
thrive on the face of the still water,
now I know why,
and my chest broke with the mystery

of the three ways the leaves were.
And the wide, yellow-cored flowers.
Inside the museum
our children stared at the mummies.
We sat in the car. I
kept seeing the stiff white petals cupping nothing,
floating there as the stems fed
up from the bottom
that wordless community, and put my head down
on the wheel, the leaves in me uttering our
cries.

from

WITH

AKHMATOVA

AT THE

BLACK GATES

Last Meeting

I was helpless, my breasts were freezing.
I walked one foot on tiptoe,
I put my left glove on
my right hand, like an idiot.

There seemed to be so many steps then
but I knew there were only three.
Autumn whispered through the maples
"Die, like me:

that sick, truculent liar, Fate,
has stripped me, for the hell of it."
"I've been flayed like you," I remember answering
as I left, "and I'll die when you do."

This is our last meeting – this place, this voice.
I looked back at the shape of the dark house.
Candles guttered in the bedroom window;
behind them, eyes and a torso.

1909

I haven't slept all night, both sides
of my pillow are damp and hot,
the second candle flame sputters
in its pool of wax, now
idiotic lewd shrieks of a crow
get closer, closer, the noise
grates on me, fills me, fills my room,
then nothing.
Everything's like that. Now
it's too late even to think about sleeping –
the white shade pulled down over the white window
is too white. Morning!
You: the same voice, the same look in your eyes
I saw when we first met, the same yellow hair.
Everything is as it was years ago –
we touched, time wasn't there.
The world passing outside my window is as clear
as the palm of my own hand; the blank,
whitewashed walls on all four sides are infinite,
are everything, are nothing. I can't think.
When I stare at them I go straight through.
The sweet, thick stink of lilies, cut minutes ago.

1911

A riding whip, a glove wait on the table,
God knows why. Who left them there?
One window's open a little.
I hear the lindens rustle.

They seem to call me.
Why did you leave? I
can't understand it. Why?
The desk lamp's cozy circle —

it focuses the pain, it lets me see again
two people shielded from the world
by love's illusion: if it lasts we can't die.
Think of us. Who were we?

Tomorrow morning's light will soothe me
like a warm hand. I know it.
I know this life is good.
Heart, don't worry —

last night I could barely hear
that hesitant, aching plea you've begun to make.
I was reading in an old book
that souls are immortal.

1914

It's here again, it moves, its tin-white scythe
flashes through the pinkish fur of tall weeds,
the *wockwock wockwock* of unshod hooves is coming closer.
Don't tell me you don't care about sleep either,
don't say you can't forget me,
can't make love in your own bed, alone now one whole year.

The moon offers its mottled, steady blade.
It stops. It makes a scar on the darkness. Darkness: the strangler.
Hoofbeats again, dream trace, memory, twin faces—us?
      —the one answer
a bitter tone in your voice, louder, louder:
sitting up all night in a chair till the sky turns white
and wakes my chilly room, I can't breathe, I see
      everything, know everything:

two or three words,
the words,
lost, like a breath,
the elation of a truth
I heard, saw, need again
but still can't quite remember.

Roses

Can you still stand on the edge of the Neva
and watch it move,
can you still walk out under the lamps and look down
from the bridges and stare until the waters blur and merge with you
and you lift your arms off the green iron railings
and shake yourself back?
I see your face above and in the water,
a man, yes, but part of me says a god;
and I still feel your mouth, opening to mine,
our tongues greeting each other;
and part of me still feels
grass, leaves, and flowers will die forever
each time snow simplifies the land.
One love, one life, one face in that river.
There's a reason I'm so sad
since the first time I saw you in a dream,
saw you hover then lie next to me in bed
then disappear like mist sucked out of my room.
Whenever you come back – more often now – I'm like a child:
angels have wings honed fine as a razor,
the end of the world is almost here – look! –
fires the size of a fist break out everywhere on the snowy hills,
blood roses puncturing that white, white skin.

Two Fragments

I wake early
from a dream of happiness that strangles me,
I look out the portholes at the waves,
green with sizzling white claws on top,
I go out on deck – there's a moon –
wrapped in a wool coat,
it drizzles as I listen to the engines mumbling,
my heart and theirs together –
I can't tell which is mine.
That way I don't need to think about anything
though I feel I'll meet you again;
I grow younger by the minute,
the salt spray, the wind slashing my face.
An image wavers before my face.

I don't see my childhood any more.
I don't see butterflies mating in air
the way I used to when I was sixteen.
Horrible how the moon spreads its chalky glow
on the sky, on the sea – town after town
poisoned, the people bent with pain:
they want death
because of the sick laws of tyrants. That's what I see.
You're gone. That's why I sing and dream.
One day I woke and the whole world was silent.
The guns had stopped.
My heart slowed, I could barely move.
Death Patrols rummaged every house except mine.

Two Little Songs

1

How many years will I live?
I asked the sparrow.
The pine tops shivered,
a narrow plank of sunlight struck the grass.
Not a sound. The raw, welcoming smell
of earth, of leaves, of whatever it is
from childhood centuries old, soaking in these woods,
and nothing else.
Now I am walking home –
a ruffle of wind cools
the tight, hot skin of my forehead.

2

I used to say nothing all morning
about what my dream told me.
For me, for the rose,
for the day's first light there's only one fate:
to be the music that is everywhere
heard *in* things, *as* things.
Snow crumbles and slides down the hills,
I'm as fragile as snow,
solid as the banks of swollen, muddy rivers –
the pungent roar of the pine thicket
is more peaceful than my thoughts at dawn.

1922

No cool breezes, not a cloud
shadowing the flat glass dome of the sky
that fall – September almost gone,
everyone shocked by its heat and color.
Thorns, roses, rocks, everything smelled heavy,
red sunsets choked the air, torturing us,
the dirty canal turned green.
We will see this until we are all dead.
The sun came back again, again, and again,
taking the capital, capturing the throne.
Sometimes nobody moved for hours.
There was a silence in which rich and poor
were one. Not a grain of dust, not a leaf lifted.
That autumn
scorched every face and brick. Whiffs of snow.
I still see one of those
moments of pure equality – I was standing next to
        a horse,
I could hear its whinnying sneezes, smell its flanks, see
a soldier's boots beneath its barrel, the back of his head where
the cap pinched his hair; links of bright metal.
I thought: I will see you until the day I die.
I went home, bathed; washed and braided my hair.
And that was when you came to my door.
I opened it. You looked at me. Your eyes
were cool and without hope like a leaf that has lost its color.

Nothingness

I want to be sick, I want to meet everyone again
in fever, I want to walk the wide streets
of the glary, seaside garden, scoured by the wind,
and forget. Nothing has happened before this.

The dead and exiled walk into my house. I want each child
brought to me by the hand. I miss them.
When I was a child my nurse's hand was always right there
above my hand. I'd reach up and clutch her finger.

I'm going to eat grapes
with the children I love, drink cold white wine,
watch the waterfall spill
bleakly over and over across my flint bed. But I still see

a house where I was taken to a cell and questioned,
led back, and I won't say what else. Now I am waking,
why am I crying, everyone loses everyone, everything.
It's done now, but my dreams – nothing

of my life in them, nothing. I do recognize ordinary things,
and rooms, people, vaguely; to be in a world completely
new is to lose everything. But I can see the waves and feel
        the sun
and smell the salt in the air that lurches and halts, gently.

I sit in my room. On the wall in front of me, the Cross.
    Nothing else.
It's as if I had never seen it before. Its hacked, blackish,
equal pieces of unstained, trashed wood hold Him up there.
        Body
of ivory. Flies land on my foot and stay there.

Memory

I'm here; it's here,
I'm not sure which is which:
sky red as a fresh knife wound, sky
of fire, abyss, my home
reviving in me after all these years
as voices, creaking wagons, the *plock*
of a butcher's cleaver passing through bone
into the block of maple,
returning from the afterlife, eternal, strange,
blood inside and out,
blood everywhere . . .

a clock face changing as the sun
circles the sky
but in me also, without hands
or numbers.

All my life
I've been terrified this would happen:
autumn:
the world, my soul —
as if everything I fought against
inside me all my life
isn't part of me now,
is the stone, leaves, flowers
of these blind walls and this small garden,
as distant as your lips are from my lips. . . .

Invisible; visible.
I don't know what the difference is.
I don't mean God, religion.
I've spent my whole life writing

clear, simple sentences, things that I felt.
Love. Loss. Bitterness. Exaltation.
But mostly tenderness –
that astonishing mood we grown-ups call "the essence of things,"
Babel says, describing how he felt as a child walking down
          his hometown streets –
no matter how hard life became, how dead
the heart felt, whipped
by its quest for love.

Impossible; possible . . .
they called my name
then took me to a wooden room.
I laughed inappropriately; a second Akhmatova went:
one peeked through neighbors' windows, picked flowers,
rambled the beach, read all day on a rock,
waves nibbling at her feet;
and one, in a chair bolted to the floor,
said anything. Anything. Or did she? Innocent. Sincere.
Like a child pacifying its mother.

Whoever I was, I'mm here now – *here* – God!
beyond my past, not there, still there
unless these homeless voices I am are
that betrayed, nameless nothingness in rags freezing
for nineteen months beside you, *you*,
prisoner, witness, women of silence – here,
Leningrad. And someone said "I can." These numb words go
like beggars, knocking at gates, and get no answer.

———

Death. Nothing. Nothing after death.
Right now when I look back over my shoulder
into the room where I sleep and write
I see my old house following me, its
one vacant, malicious, hollow eye

of light all night long gnawing through the wall, the darkness.
Fifteen years. Forever. Dense as granite.
Akhmatova: Granite: Time:
the verge of revelation – that the past
can't be held or measured, that it changes,
that it's as strange to me as it would be
to my neighbor if he could see it, hear it, taste it.

Late one night
I couldn't sleep. I dressed and went outside and stretched out
        in the cold grass
behind my house
where the dry, scrambled, black stalks clicked,
tangling against the sky, and the barn hulks stood out,
        infinitely serene,
the entire world far in the distance –
stars, clouds.
What were those cores of light, that surf of yearning formlessness
doing there, what were they trying to say?
I thought I could hear them speaking to me

it was the voice of millions,
a voice above our meeting,
a voice muttering nothing I understood
to the one I left,
as if my own voice stunned me when it came
from God knows where, one uninterrupted, unidentified scream....

———

There's a house, I'm not sure where.
In it fine, brown dust has thickened on everything,
in it the woman I was still clings to the man
who could have killed me, we were so close,
I was so young and lost in my love for him.
That flat, grayish-brown light of just-before-winter
still dulls things there, a sign of nonexistence.

And there are times, writing this, trying to know
what to say, when whole pages
from unsent letters fill my head
as if the only life I really have is in the truth of passion
I can never let you know . . .

wind enters the chimney and it sounds like me
or like the person in those letters
or like all the changes made in these lines
or like the men and women who still march back
to that house where . . .

what good are details?

————

An inkstain
no one bothered to wipe off
my bleached oak dining-room table,
a kiss
so hard I still feel bone against bone at times, again, again
          until I believe
love *is* eternal, love is the one law,
the same spider I saw in that house
motionless on its web right there
across from me as I say this and reach to touch . . .

the clock, a tear, these moments of you. . . .

I'm awake now:
shame, anger, inescapable revenge.
The road that led to me here
unrecognizable. Nobody knows us.
The city burns, old fires sputter out, finally,
1942. With a lamp and a bunch of keys
glittering before me, I sit at my desk, I see
the one witness I trust: my thin, crippled maple
looking in at this woman speaking,

knowing we won't meet again, offering
its dried-out, scrawny arms to me.
Tobruk rumbles through the floor
into my legs and spine and hands,
one unexpected, pure, white star looks – yes, looks –
      and sees me,
sitting alone,
not only me but everyone
who suffers with its distant, steady, pitiless way
of being here.

City I love, we'll never be apart –
when I leave, my shadow will cling to your walls,
my breasts and face tremble in your canals,
my footsteps sound in the museums,
I'll cut a path by pacing some green field
as I walk and walk, free, kneeling over the silence
of the graves my brothers lie in,
seeing their faces, tasting their tears.

The unknowable sleep of things embraces the world.
Everyone looks through a strange window.
Some live in Tashkent, some in Philadelphia
in this age of sickening, bitter air,
the air of exiles and poisons. I left –
bridges, tunnels, the Kama lidded with ice –
I took the road so many from this country died on:
my son, you, you, and you, a live, huge knotted thread
being dragged through the grim, crystal silence of Siberia
by filthy gods.
The sleep of things. What is it? Sunset or dawn,
the maple still looks in. Nobody's there, or here. Keys
      on the desk.
The woods are quiet. A handful of camp dust. This
woman still being questioned by men in uniform; this
blued revolver lifted so many times to her head –

one's own voice heard always as a miracle, each step
and detail of the world, each instant of consciousness impossible . . .

I speak to the city from the other side,
not Hell or Heaven, but not from where you are,
one woman, one man, and millions,
I, who discovered how to forget even love,
who could sit looking at the ocean for weeks – there were no days –
     waiting
for the one who could split open even wider my terrified
     heart.

————

Photograph: families looking of all things shy
cupping their genitals with both hands
so we will never see – doesn't that mean they
still knew their own names?
grouped on the edge of the bottom half of the shot
that could be of the deep gray ocean
a pit that does not end with the shot
but flows out past its edges in the mind
as they try not to be there by looking as if nothing special
is going on
huddling in front of the amateur Sunday photographer's candid
visor-shaded blank eye

Photograph: whole bodies of bubbling wounds flung
across torsos down thighs like frozen cloth over backs faces
a patch of boiling skin so abstract
its patterns are your mother's face
or animals or an arm of twilit Cape Cod beach
embracing smooth water

Photograph: silent cloud mushrooming on your fat stem
caught swallowing whatever lived beneath you

the newsreel slows
how amazing harmless and beautiful you are in silence
as you blossom and rise and take everything with you
in the murky theatre on the screen.

————

To feel another's pain—
as a passenger in an airplane for the first time hesitates
to look out the porthole
then looks, because being afraid is childish, and sees the earth as
a wrinkled map interrupted by clouds, merely beautiful—
is, I suppose, human. Girlish, harmless, and beautiful.

If we stay up this far long enough we will stop on the moon.
The prisoners' faces glow like the moon
on any night in almost any weather—
in the photographs, though a few plead
or grimace or leer or seem to be finishing an urgent sentence—
heads jutting, eyes wide, half-smiling, half-open mouths—
the rest look drained of feeling, their faces ashen,
their souls fully resigned,
convinced,
surrendered to the endlessness of death,
abandoned by all of us.
They lean out at us,
their gray, ascetic faces
a shade darker than new snow,
than that star I saw watching us.

And what we know is
those God tore away from us
get along very well without us
until, until

————

In my book, *Plantain*,
I said I kept silent for weeks,
I sat on a stone by the sea,
"my last tie with the sea is broken,"
I saw the reddish moon
enter the branches of a single pine, pass through,
be there again between twigs, needles, until

you stood near me,
glimmer of identity, soul,
whatever makes men free,

we touched, we became one voice

like a lover on whose face
the sad accident of moonlight continues.

New Year's

O it's so haggard, the face of the moon! Blurry
with clouds, it gilds each bleak slope of the hill
in papery light. Six places at my table
and one, only one empty –

my husband and I and out friends
celebrating, seeing the New Year in.
Why are my fingers stained with blood?
The wine scorches my throat. Why?

The host picks up his glass; it's full.
The host is very serious, doesn't move.
"Drink to the soil of our own forests,
drink to the clearings, where we lie."

Trees. Whenever I catch a glimpse of them
at the window, I stop listening, look away, I see
them and the moon as one, one old, pale,
truthful, speechless couple, at peace.

My face. One of my friends
studies it and sees, remembers – God knows what –
and shouts "Drink to her lines,
drink to the poems, where we live."

And one steps out into the night, unable
to understand, and waits in the piney darkness
and looks up and, reading my mind, calls back to us
"Drink to the one who still is not with us."

Thread

I rake the hotbed straw,
I look left half a mile downhill
where the dull green pond

shimmers. Dirt circles it, a raw, wide swath.
Even from this far I can see
creamy scum squirming inside

along the edge. The pond's a squarish oval.
Lamps, chairs, books: what's man-made barely has a smell.
I think I hear a little boy singing,

I think of the blackness of night, of one
especially when you never came back.
My face still feels like your face, when I think of you.

A chill floats in.
I've piled daisies in every corner of the house,
heaped vegetables in bowls, on tables;

you gone, this silence – it will never end –
my lines desolate – they can't reach you;
now the deep blue shape of each lapel is

here again as I stitch them onto the notched collar,
now the brass, eagle-figured buttons, stripes, insignia,
the weeks it took to finish, weeks when snow

stopped, fell, stopped then fell, fell endlessly:
red splashes, frozen mules, my needle whisking thread
through wool, air, sky . . . even God!

How can I write unless your dying guides my hand.
Touch me. Snow makes the silence ominous, holy. Not a flake
      is mine.
No story, no elegy. Nothing to explain.

All I need is to tell you —
without hope, without fear, in one cold line —
28 bullet holes in the last uniform I sewed.

Tashkent Blossoms, 1944

This city is all light, as if a king
waved his hand and was obeyed. Every window throbs with it,
    every street.
I look up into it, I live.
Is it real? How can we eat when there's war, how can we live?

The anxious breath of mothers is easier to understand
than what they say. These days I see
so many of them kissing their children, see
our pocked, useless fields and gutted houses.

If you sit still, don't move, don't say anything,
you'll hear the last of the railroad guns lobbing
shells seventy-five miles into those fields,
see children playing in craters three storeys deep.

But I will see
crisp, twisted, brown-crusted rolls of bread shining
in the hands of young mothers even after I die.
They fed their children. They had long, clean hair.

1945

Lynx-eyed Asia, you looked into my soul
and saw something – secret, sacred, furious,
it tortures me
like the heat at noon in Termezsk.
You teased it out.
Silence hums in its veins – it *is* silence –
that noiselessness in bed in the dark
just after a mosquito passes, comes back
and buzzes in your ear –
here before us, it will always be here:
Being: all that's left
in the eyes of the homeless, jailed, defenseless ones
without family:
what God is to us in this century.
God, when we pray to you, pray to us,
prove we need each other, live the way we do,
come down and share – when we have nothing more to say –
what it is to be human, what it is
to live in this dying country.
Each taste of love I've ever had oozes
into my conscience like lava
simmering beneath my door.
Crackling, spitting it breaks in.
I drink every one of my own tears from invisible hands.

This Cold

The skis won't creak again
on the dry snow –
a scowling moon pinned to a blue sky,
the gently steepening meadow –I know, I know.

Windows are faces in the distance.
I can't find a track or a path,
only the black ice holes go anywhere.
It's good here.

The snow is like a simple wedding gown.
Ski tracks cross it – stitches –
and the image of us risking ourselves one night
hand in hand years back returns.

Now nothing but this cold, these walls, this snow,
this ordinary place, this patient mind.
I see whatever is here, in front of me, inside me;
I don't look beyond.

Anyone who sees my eyes
knows that immediately and feels
heavier than a parent staring into its dead
child's eyes, and sees

memory: a stone at the bottom of my soul.
Men change to things, conscious, brutal things
that kill. My sorrow's everywhere
because you're a memory, because you're lost.

The roof of stars will never go out.
I wish I were ill. I am very calm.
This life is so glorious I could even forget
the night we went crazy and lay down next to each other in the snow.

You

Each minute what I hear is you –
summer, winter –
when I sit down to write.
Now the sky is blue, blue, transparent glass,
sea-blue where the sea, down to the placid floor, is clear.
Someone practices the guitar,
someone writes. But who?
This perfect, blank page *was*
perfect and blank minutes ago.
I look out the window at the sea;
it changes; it stays the same;
no one paces the dunes.
Reeds. Gray hollows. Whitecaps. My ragged braids.
Snow hoods the grasses; the trees look dead; I hear
men yelling at the sheep, a child's cry,
cedars thrashing outside my door.
Love's nothing, love is
what a schoolgirl hopes will prove she's beautiful
when she's alone.

These days before spring I'm amazed at how light my body is,
I don't even recognize my own house:
that instrument, that breeze, those men, water –
coming from nowhere, going nowhere –
enter me like my breath.
I watch the black-limbed alder.
Sun splashes through it like wine from a pitcher.
And God?

I see myself, and you –
one face in the mirror, seeking us, younger, at sunrise
or at night, kissing, the wet of our mouths one mouth,
our whole bodies touching – and hear:

"You wouldn't sleep with me. You wouldn't let me kiss your breasts.
You were stupid; afraid; beautiful; you knew nothing.
Day and night are the same. I can't find a letter,
not one word we spoke remains. Couldn't you see
the ghosts we were, even then? Didn't you know
we'd disappear?"

Fragment, 1959

And entering towns the guns had missed,
towns out of storybooks,
we saw the constellation of the Snake
but we were afraid to look at each other.

The earth smelled like an orphanage – potatoes,
disinfectant, shoes – I believed faceless
Time walked beside us: years, centuries.
And someone shook a tambourine, someone we couldn't see.

There were noises and tiny bluish-yellow lights.
What did they mean, those fireflies
signaling to us, beckoning? We stopped.
I even thought those noises were the lights.

Then we walked on together. I was with you, you were with me.
It was like that dream I had: the corpse of an old man
shone in the dark, a baby clung to his chest, both wrapped in a cocoon.
I could see the twitchy, delicate, wax-like hands of the baby

dabbling at the man's chin. The moon slid out,
suddenly. We met, we said goodbye.
If you remember that night, as I do,
wherever you are now, whatever fate

steers your life, know what I know: the time
we had was sacred like a great king's dream
turned by his people into a myth they use
to keep from believing life is a dream.

Whatever I looked at was alive, everything had a voice,
but I never found out: were you a friend, an enemy,
was it winter, summer? Smoke, singing, midnight heat.
I wrote thousands of lines. Not one told me.

In the Evening

1

I almost never think about you, I don't care
what happens to you now, but the wound of our meetings
hasn't healed. I still walk past your red house in the sun
above the muddy river where you live peacefully.

On blue evenings I try to predict the future
like a witch. I have a feeling we'll meet again.
Two monks pass slowly along the top of an old castle wall.
All day the bells have tolled over the endless, plowed fields.

2

There's a line between people, a secret margin that being in love
or passion can't cross even when lips bite each other
and the heart is smashed by love, in pure silence. It's unbearable!

Friendship can't do anything there,
neither can the years of fiery, narrow happiness
when the soul's free and doesn't feel the slow boredom of flesh.

Anyone who tries to cross that line is insane,
those who reach it are punished by despair.
Now you know why your hands don't cover my breasts.

3

I almost never dream about you now,
I don't see you the way I used to, everywhere,
mist has blocked off the white road,
shadows keep jumping across the water.

I'm cutting off all the branches of the lilac bushes
that don't have flowers. I want
the tame, knowable, physical world that can't see me.
God has cured me with the icy calm of not loving.

Alone

No one can hurt me. They've tried to kill me
so many times that nobody scares me now.
I know what kind of people want me dead:
fanatics in love, political, dressed up to look poor.
Nothing they can do is hidden from me.
This ordinary room of mine
is Paradise, cut off, a stone box
that overlooks my old street, people I used to know.
There's so little in it – two chairs,
bed, table, books, a red Persian prayer rug
with a cross in a golden field in the middle.
It could be called a trap; maybe it is.
But what I feel
is gratitude – to those who put me here
and, in their way, hung doors, cemented brick, glazed windows;
may they never be ill or worried; may life pass them by.
I'm up this morning with the workers, I see
my face in the streaked mirror, bleached with anxiety,
and what I am is what the sun is –
itself free of itself daily
even when its last shard of light eases under the rim of the earth.
Everything's dark. Whenever I shut my eyes.
I look outside; turn back;
look in the mirror and see
the small window, reflected:
pines miles away across a field,
a road, one cloud, clumps of bluish mist, some dead machine
slouched in a gown of rust – nature, things dropping back to nature,
me noticing my face among it all.
I tie one short ribbon in my gray hair
and step back – so much younger than the face I see –
nowhere, homeless, peaceful,

and speak to the voice inside me that answers me.
Sometimes I only sit here. Winds from a frozen sea
come through the open window. I don't get up, I
don't close it. I let the air touch me. I begin to freeze.
Twilight or dawn, the same pink streaks of cloud.

A dove pecks wheat from my extended hand,
those infinite, blind pages, stacked on my table . . .

some desolate urge lifts my right hand, guides me.
Much much older than I am, it comes down,
easy as an eyelid, godless, and I write.

Endings

I can barely speak
but I still have things to say;
not being in love is a relief.
There's nothing between me and the sky;
it starts at the hills, it shelters everything, it
goes on and on.
I think. I plan. With purity.
Books, paperweights, bunches of old drafts
flow with the world, flow with what's in my mind.
Not to withhold oneself is clarity.
Not to need safety
as the nothingness grows. . . .

These nights I sleep.
Insomnia nurses someone else.
When I look back to find *him*, to see *it*,
nothing's there. The black
iron hands on the tower clock
aren't arrows now.
That's how it is: everything is what it is – light.
I'm free, I forgive, forgive all, I live
without beliefs, looking at the sun – past dawn now –
flash on patches of wet ivy until it blinds me.

Dandelions like words follow a low wood fence.
Some cluster against a post, some stray between.
One story ends, another begins,
mine, yours, everyone's.
And fear: each brick on each pale house looks paler,
nothing is warm;
an ambulance's crazed, multiple wail
drifts in on fog and incense,
me re-creating this, believing this, being this

as if she and I were the same,
speaking in my third-floor room.

Don't you see us on the shelled road that May night?
Each inch in front of us was a wall.
The ditches whispered. Carnations. I thought
all Asia smelled like that –
blood, steel carcasses, fire –
but I was hallucinating, happiness
broke like a flare above the trenches,
war forced it into my soul,
war and the craziness of love.

Now autumn eats its way in. Wild frilly
puffs of mildew staining a wall, ecstasy, tenderness,
glances, a handshake or brown leaf –

anything could end this:
who is it, I or you?

I lift my face – close; closer.
The phrases blur, the blur
rises from silence into silence,
each syllable echoing,
each touch a resurrected meaning.
I roll this page backwards in the machine
to make it disappear, then spin it back
and see the emptiness around, between
each letter, word, and line.
I feel the eyes of whatever is here
watch me. I watch what watches me.

Books packed on sagging shelves, the unending red brick houses
of my childhood, of my life now, row on row,
where a bum sits whittling
on a neighbor's steps, yards piled with bedsprings,
legless chairs, branches the poor are saving.

I move my lips.
The sky is a hard blue.
Death's death. There's no sleep at the end,
no waking as I woke to these words –
don't you see us? –
no bringing-back to life. Only this voice,
continuing here above Mt. Vernon Street,
only these accidental words.
I listen.

Don't you see us – a soul, a brightness?

On the wall day
splashes a pane of light. Through it
we are taken.

from

IN IT

Leaves

More and more often as the years accumulate,
the life you are living inside you rises until it *is* you.
The moon, that ruined badge of lovers,
looks beautiful again, rueful, large;
the vacant street, dotted with garbage,
seems to be lighted differently, from within,
and death – *it happens, it can't but it will, when?*
to you – is merely a fact you don't need explained.
It begins one night usually: one, then another.
Behind trees, leaves bickering between houses,
people drift in their rooms.
One works at a sink, one reads, one
sweeps, one faces you, his anonymous head motionless,
you step to the window, stay, try to let him know
you know he's fixed across the way
watching you, daydreaming, waiting – for what?
Night is a pool of heat filling your breast,
a bearable, steady fear throbbing with images
that makes your nipples rise and will not cool.
Maybe you accept what seeps into you
to become you, deepening into itself.
Maybe the unconsoling stars, vapid, white,
like the eyes of massive, unnamed animals,
those black leaves struggling on a wall,
know. But a mindless voice
that has its passion, has its hunger, keeps
thrusting like an extra heart,
grows more like the actual touch
of hands and lips,
grows closer to the one you feel is you,
is you, is you, here,
in the flesh, *your* flesh, now.

The Rocks

The cold is here. Impossible to wake
those browns, greens, streaks of purple and gray
with spray from the hose, its nozzle plugged with ice,
impossible to enjoy
those faces, tangled in lily stalks and weeds.
One summer Sunday, wearing old sneakers,
Bill and I drove to the Wissahickon
and slid down the embankment to the creek,
soaking our pants as we knelt to pick out good ones,
rolling, lifting, cradling, cursing
as we kicked steps up the steep mushy sides
and stumbled out
and dropped them in the trunk,
then after five or six trips planted them here.
I loved kneeling on them stiff-armed with all my weight,
snugging them tighter into the dirt,
hearing the gritty shifting until each one fit.
Their muddy, unashamed aloneness,
their permanent, homely sorrow soothed me.
My favorite is right out of Buson's six-panel screen:
fierce, haggard, recklessly free, floating in air
or earthless, simply there,
a few touching, merging, all thirteen
brushed in a kind of accidental
poise without meaning or purpose.
The sketchy translucent strokes seem to tremble –
you can see through them – as if our fear of time, death, how
temporary we are is what the rocks are.
He lay the screen on the floor.
Just above it was a window clouds would glide across.
He'd look up at the clouds, then paint. Look up. Paint.
Drink wine late afternoons, watching the sun slip away.
Spend some days only leaning over it,

scouring its five-by-eleven whiteness,
unfocusing, lost in it, imagining
shapes live, shapes die,
flicking the dry bristles unconsciously with his thumb, not knowing
when, where – four months from his death –
the next rock would appear, bending abruptly,
filling, wielding his short-handled brushes faster and faster until
the ink ran out. Snow now,
gentle, wispy, far-apart, helpless flakes
the tiniest breeze gusts back up or shoots across,
then calm, and then they float straight down
slow, very slow. How good it seems,
exactly like late spring afternoons picnicking by the river –
long after people had finished eating,
wife, daughters, friends stretched on the grass talking,
forks, spoons, leftovers packed away – I'd stand, and, looking
beyond heads across the water, shake out our tablecloth
again again again
until my arms hurt and I couldn't hear,
then fold it into a white square,
drop it on the lidded wicker basket.
Day end. Blue wisps of light skimming the treetops.
        I remember thinking
trees, grass – their silence – that's probably why
we go to them, touch them, stare
as I did by the river –
unattached phrases, rhymes, half called-out images, "of time,
        death, how"
happening in my mind like whipcracks –
then at dusk I turned and lay with my family,
grass damp and cool,
geese massed for bread along the banks,
everything in shadow, shadow everywhere.

Visiting the Stone

Last week on my way to the shrink between connections
the drunk who's always sprawled on the El stop steps –
emaciated fingers, rags, bruised stumps –
pointed to his ankles where his feet should be
and shook a paper cup. I popped in a quarter,
stepped over his legs,
then caught the bus to my appointment.
For years I've been asking "Why?" "How?"
unraveling this story and that,
but what can explanation or advice do
when the answers don't apply?
This afternoon for the first time since they
set the stone ten years ago, unpolished gray Vermont granite
embellished with a three-inch etched border
of bare vines, I knelt at my father's grave,
memorizing his dates chiseled in the marker,
and asked him, too,
then brushed off clusters of dried pine needles, dirt-streaks,
in the field of dwarfish stones. *You*
his voice flashed like a scar on air
its cold, useless answer.

To Charlie

A broom, its straws bleached, tips bent, leans
against a green plastic hose coiled
on the side of the house above the drain,
every few seconds one
slow long drop slips from the nozzle,
yellow, orange, and blue lilies stick out between
rocks Bill and I hauled from the Wissahickon
at least five years ago. Now
we're fifty, now in a letter from Charlie—
"One can get terribly frightened of age, aging."
What was it yesterday that made me so happy?
For one instant—no
people, street, sky, ominous glass buildings—
I stood there, not a thought or question,
no trace of the inevitable "Why?"
that loves giving its bitterness to me.

Both

It's almost a month since we touched, or wanted to,
that's why I bought these dense, yellow-headed flowers.
All the way home
I kept putting my nose to the chopped stem-ends
that soaked in the grocer's pail and held the scent of earth.
Dry now after a week, still bright on our kitchen table,
they fan out of the vase I stuck them in.
Each day a few petals drop to the varnished wood.

Monet's *Cloud, 1903*, is nearly all water
but at the top a narrow chunk of the pond's bank
is a sky of shaggy weeds.
Upside down in the water two clouds float:
one's crisp, tight; one's fuzzy, larger.
Lemon and pink lilies glow on their pads,
sitting in the life I envy;
at the bottom two white ones jut out,
taller than the others, surrounded by heavy leaves.

Some nights, trying to kill what haunts us, what is us,
we scream at each other until we can't speak.
Our skin can't bear the touch of the other's hand.
We sleep on the edges of our bed.
The clouds in the middle of the water, going nowhere,
don't know what's happening to us either.

What is happening?
A full moon eases across our window.
We stare at each other across the table
who have lived together so many years
hearing the vein-blue echoings of self-in-the-other
flushed by the terrified, helpless child within
until it shows itself when we stand close,

clear as the thin oil and tiny hair
of each pore of our faces.

Two blue-white strokes rush through the painting and stay there,
raised slashes of anger, scars, troubling the scene.

The twine you tied from the rusted iron socket outside
the kitchen window to the drainpipe has broken.
The vines you planted months ago have pulled it down.
They lie woven in each other at our feet, flame-blue
morning glories pointing in all directions,
slim yellow throats and dusty tongues
silent, gaping with hunger.

Trash trapped under tires, envelopes ripped across one edge,
newspapers flapping on a fallen beam, sky
through the glassless windows of a shell,
a mattress, its black intestinal springs and poor, coarse hair drooling
from a gash, stray green weeds poked through, the intact parts
        of its ticking pooled with stains —

the back door open behind us, we stand side by side absolutely
        still, knuckles so close their warmth touches,
the moon, stalled across from the sun at this hour, dawn,
        a translucent, pitted eye.

Last Elegy

Surgeons cutting a hole
in my father's skull
with one of those saws that lift
a plug out of bone also took
a big lump off my spine
in the dream I don't understand
that flickered back
the day before he died.
We were at the shore following
a golf match on TV,
eating, napping. His drained
gray face didn't reveal
any sense of being here,
any desire to live.
The money he made,
the failure he thought he was
in love, in business,
intensified his mood
after the heart attack.
The sky blew flat, smeary gray,
a few fly-like figures
paced the cold beach. Millie,
Clair, Margot, Mom and I
didn't know how to stop his
staring out of nothing into nothing,
so we watched hard
Nicklaus miss two easy putts
and other famous pros tee off
with that quick fluid swing
they have, then stroll down
the fairway to the ball,
the entire world manicured, green.

To say "I love you"
meant "I know I'm dying."
but you said it,
at least I think I heard you
whisper it to me. Or was it to yourself?
I kept my eyes on the screen.

Three Voices

FOR CHARLIE

I

Late one night – one of those mild, hazy nights
just before Christmas – elated, buzzing with wine,
I dialed the house you were renting on Laguna Beach.
No answer. I imagined you
gazing until it got light –
phosphorescent whitecaps skittering through darkness,
faint lines of code loaded with meaning,
dissolving at your feet.

I needed talk about poetry, women, one of those talks
when we say anything to find
insight, truth – lost instantly: you feel it, see it, can't say
     what it is –
its doomed, wordless afterimage stabbing the air.
We've no identity then,
we're anyone, anything – faces, walls,
windows vacant and stark, words on a page,
is, is quavering in every cell.

I sat in my kitchen with the lights off,
hearing Giacometti's despair –
in his *Notebooks* he writes he couldn't sculpt a head
the way he saw it, "the way it is,"
but it wasn't only that.
He couldn't believe consciousness includes death, *his* death:
"He goes on speaking, but he's dead . . . is he dead?"
seeing himself awake at the moment of death,
suffering what James warns in his story
about the fear of love becomes "the horror of waking."

A skinny, agonized, bent, bronze arm perched on a steel rod,
its hand splayed, is Giacometti's scream,

corkscrewing up through your chest into your throat and out
when no one else is there –
the aloneness of life,
how strange and miraculous it is,
how it simply is, how all is.

Tonight is another night like that.
This desk, this lamp, this paper, these too familiar hands.
In a cone of light below me
a man in a loose, brown, buttonless overcoat
hacks with a handax a sawed-off chunk of branch pinned
      under his foot,
making short pieces, splinters, stacking them against a wall
of the shack he sleeps in in somebody's yard.
Each time he slashes the ax down breath
puffs from his lips the way words bud, blossom
between us and immediately die. . . .

    2
"Do you ever think about yourself?"
A kind, unindulgent shrink I knew
answers, "Almost never. . . ."
In Princeton, years later,
a teacher from Japan, a short man dressed in a shiny gray suit,
asks, after I tell him I'm in pain,
"Who is the I?"
twists his right hand like a corkscrew
above his head and says, "This is the sharpest sword
      in the world –
it can cut anything – can it cut itself?"
"No. No. No. Be the sword!" I blurt out.
Sitting next to me in the stuffy third-floor office,
my friend Jeff growls, "Of course it can!" Adamant, sure.
"The ego has no foundation, you know . . ." the teacher says.
I stand: "I'm standing here – on the *floor!*"
"Show me where you're standing," he says.
I hesitate, look down, step back, and point to where I *was*

and we start laughing. "Why didn't you do *this*?" I hear,
and he walks toward me, stops, his breath warm on my face,
his eyes my eyes, my eyes his, for
one split second nothing mine.

3
This morning, waiting for the 33
a block from the halfway house near my house:
one of those old, moronic baby-men
who lounge in the sun on a bench all day
or scrounge candy wrappers, pennies, butts, then ring
your doorbell for a quarter, skips up to me,
leans on me, tilts his head, smiles up at me
and I ask Do you ever take the bus? *No No* he utters,
shaking his head, *No! No!* Do you ever go downtown? *Oh*
        No No No
he answers, urgent, sure. *Can't even find my mother*
he confesses, solemnly. How old are you? *Sixteen. . . .*
His toothless, wizened bag of a face, adolescently shy,
points down at the pavement to avoid me, to escape being seen,
as the bus comes and the doors fold open
and I hop up and in, on the reeling floor,
squeezed between a fat black lady clutching a Bible,
hugging a pole with her free arm, and a man with a curly,
        stiff red beard
who flashes his age card at the driver.
Poor sweet little guy – shod in white socks, blue plastic
        shower shoes
squashed at the heels – he shuffles back
to his brothers and sisters, stops, turns, waves at me
following him through the bus window as we pull away
No No Oh No No No No No

The Visit

At the clear heart of the paperweight in green,
carved, pastel ice
where you'd expect a village snow scene
whose flakes twirl and fall when you shake it
is *Don't Forget Your Mother!*
Nothing moves. The message floats there,
a heart-shaped fan opens behind it,
cheap greeting-card pink. Thin as hair
a few black abstract flourishes
as if scratched by a nervous fingernail
hang here and there like Heidegger's "thought paths."
It used to be in the city, now it sits
on a teak end table by a window
in my mother's condo at the shore,
clouds, roofs, unrecognizable domestic things,
the sea, glittering in it.
Right now she cleans,
dusting knickknacks and shelves. I watch from a chair.
Sweet whiffs of bacon, toast, eggs, coffee. "Reaaady!"
Mouth open, too, at twenty,
arms raised in terror or surprise,
on the table
in an oval silver frame
up to my waist in surf, in black and white, I
yell toward some lost face on the beach
whose unrelenting timeless absence echoes.

And the Scream

The thirtyish, Irish, red-nosed carpenter
who works for Coonan—he rehabs houses up here—
is already half stoned on beer
before eight and chases his son past my front window,
screaming at him, the kid's glasses,
thick as my little finger,
bobbling on his nose.
Thin steady pewter drizzle,
long smudges yellowing the sky,
clouds darkening the street abruptly,
Pat and Jack Laurent's house gloomy
across from mine (they're away), even the embroidery
of lace curtains, the high-
arched Victorian double doors
incapable of lightening the mood.
That boy disappearing between houses
reminds me of when I
punched my whole arm through the glass door
between our dining room and kitchen
(my mother wouldn't leave it open)
and gashed my elbow so it bled on the floor
big splashes and wouldn't stop
and my mother's or my
scream seemed to echo everywhere. That boy—
from my living room one night, in the dark,
I watched his father screaming, waving a beer bottle
above the mother stretched out in a slip in bed under
a hatless four-bulb ceiling fixture's neutral blue-white glare.
Nobody would call this poetry.
When I leaf through serious books, though, I see
blindings, suicides, revelations,
some lust that breeds disaster.
Families and blood are what we want—
because we need love or can't love?

For example, my mother tells me (we're face-to-face in her
        living room,
she will not look at me when she speaks)
her mother had to pick lice from her scalp when she was ten,
her piano-prodigy Christian Scientist brother
refused help from a doctor so he died at twenty-six,
coughing blood into a bucket while she watched. Poor. Crazy.
And so on, and so on, and therefore—
incomplete sentences, true,
sketches merely,
like watching a scream through glass, as I have twice lately,
filling in the detail of hearing
plus all the other crap: motives, stupidities,
money, sex, "the real reason," someone always dying.
But what I need to say is—
Yes, merely a sketch, that's it,
that's us, half-known, unredeemable animals,
and the scream, the scream.

In Blue Light

Stealing a dollar once just before dawn
from my father's thick wallet on the dresser
while he slept, I saw how innocent he was
facing the ceiling, not seeing anything.
Four or five feet away my mother lay on her side.
Tie clip, key ring, loose change
shifted while I teased it out
and watched his things grow clearer in blue light:
Trojans, their foil packets glinting,
business cards, the hanky from his jacket pocket
still folded, clean, white. Why was I there?
His eyes twitched, relaxed, he snorted
once, twice, three, with the last inch of the money –
clinkings, breaths –. I was twelve.
Minutes later, waiting in the bright street, I thought
back to their bodies, to the boy-ghost hovering there, and
fist in my pocket, crushed the bill,
then pulled it out and let the gutter have it.

The Voice

Older girls taunted me into one of those
apartment-house basement window wells;
I crouched in that waist-high hole,
hoping they'd go away. Like a bunch of birds
pecking at crumbs they'd flirt and try to kiss me.
After they'd had their fun I'd talk to myself down there,
my Dad's flat, gravelly voice was mine,
a twin, bodiless soul
echoing against moist cement walls.
There are quaint streaks of noise inside my head
that are him talking, sometimes cursing the beautiful
mistake of life, sometimes asking how I am –
memory, I guess, but who knows, maybe
it's really him, yearning because he's lonely,
my grouchy old man asking me to a movie,
how the children are, about money,
"How's the poetry business?" – maybe
it is the rich ash of his bones and flesh
learning to speak again.

Summer Twilight

Sitting here,
doing nothing,
I let my open hands
find the warm stone step
the way I'd touch a woman
for the first time,
I look up and see
the street lamps flare,
men drifting to their stoops
to finish a drink,
bask in the peaceful weather,
small figures in calm air.
On a smooth white wall
I think I see
a shadow judging me,
shaky, familiar, thin,
that can show up anywhere
any time it decides,
its weightless life
like the silence in a room
after lovers
have talked, made love, talked again
and, shorn of purpose,
drifted off to sleep.
In an earlier place
the boy I think I was
would stay out late
waiting for the ice truck –

no one really exists
no one's to blame
running through his mind—
then when it parked for deliveries
he'd scoop loose daggers
off the tailgate, stand there
chewing until his teeth hurt.

Sad Invective

The man who sold his business to a business is looking for a business.
I went to high school with him, we played ball, he was a
                great second base.
Let's say he made eight million on the deal, selling his Dad's
                Brixite factory – that's what I heard –
and can't find anything exciting to do. Let's say he's used up pleasure.
What happens when you reach the end of money, is it like being sent
                to bed, age three, before you got tired?
You'd lie up there in the lonely dark, listening to the grown-ups,
trying to pick up from their dull static of words
your name, stories about the real world.
Do you ever feel the way I do: wanting money after fucking, money
before eating, money in handmade envelopes under the bed, money
stitched to your thighs, money that can't run out?
Man's first cure for the poison of error was money.
Having a lot of money means everyone loves you, you can't die.
And pain is beautiful when you're rich.
And even being sick is fun. Let's consider this a religious question,
immortality in the fantasy of being fed by the double mother,
of never being afraid of anyone – no academic deans, no Presidents
                great at fund-raising, no strict English Department Chairmen –
imagine being what hunger dreams it wants.
Everything's backwards in my mind.
The worker doesn't want to be boss, not much.
The boss doesn't love the girl curving in worship at his feet, not
                much.
I don't want oil deeds piled like shirts in my dresser, not much.
Work hard, don't get sick, do everything just right
or we'll put you away with the other crazies,
don't be different, don't be quite you, want, want, want,
lie back, bask in the unbroken warmth of money –
all this, forgive me, because a high school friend pocketed
                eight million bucks, I hear,
and won't be happy until he gets more, more.

One

You stood up in a dream
yelling at me not to envy
the plush chairs, silver, crystal
in a rich man's dining room,
smiling a little
as you reached to touch me.
Even after I shaved and ate
your echo came.
Since then my voice is colder, gruff,
I've noticed you don't smile
in snapshots, but withdraw
into the dead void of yourself
beyond, where no one is,
except in one: playing shuffleboard
on a cruise ship to Havana
in the late Thirties.
You sport wide flannel pants
that flare violently,
immaculate, bright white flags
faded by the shot's age.
Passengers line the deck,
asleep in slatted chairs
or amused by the game
and, as the puck (blurred inches from your stick)
takes off, you twist sideways,
facing the camera, grinning,
as if you knew I'd be here
to speak to you.
But it's the thick hardwood disc
that ended who knows where
your aim sent it I hear —

clacking others apart,
nosing up to a bunch,
missing them all, sliding
across the court lines
in its lone silence.

In Washington Square

There's a man
who sits on a bench in the park nearby
and holds his arm across his eyes all day.
Sometimes he gets up and sits on the grass and stares down
as if he's pondering a hole
and would die if he turned away,
like someone who keeps checking himself in mirrors
to see if he exists.
He raises his arm to stay alive, he believes,
not against the sun, or me, or anything,
he's protecting the world from himself, and himself
from being gone, and God from seeing him.

Today, walking to work, I passed him in his frail, grisly clothes
and lifted my arm to sense
what it's like to be in pure fear.
Crickets ticked in the park. The fountain's thick, lusty plume
gushed and swayed, squirrels rode the branches.
On my way home, there he was again, cross-legged on the grass,
head down, growling how God's not infinite, not perfect,
not everywhere, not beautiful, not, not, not,
and, like us, can't be known, and (who knows why)
an essay about fish that bite each other's mouths
before they copulate came to mind: the female
sticks her eggs on the side of a rock and the male
glides across, fertilizing them, then both
gulp mouthsful of sand and squirt it to slice trenches
the eggs will rest in. The white eggs
brocade the rock like a cloud of pearls
sewn on the bodice of a gown. Twilight –
a lullaby of cars and water,
the peace of illusion –

he began to rock, *davening* the Jews call it, death motion,
the fluctuating drone of the griever,
the darker it got the faster he rocked, back and forth back and forth,
the hypnotic frayed thread of his cry
coming from nowhere.

A God

Alone at night in my room,
typing these words,
baffled by what they will be
as evening blackens a patch of moss on a tree trunk,
chandeliers of brown seeds, stuttering birds,
I go back:
my daughters chat about school
or I'm reciting that great short poem *The Wind Shifts*,
catching pain in a student's eyes,
and I can't tell whose life is mine.
In yellow light a woman dusts a table
then sits reading for awhile.
In the alley a dog squats. Its master
hobbles out on crutches, stands by, watches,
and as I try these lines,
whispering to myself, to anyone, to you,
a pale shadow in a nightgown
appears in the kitchen doorway.
Light winks between her thighs
where the bare curves almost meet,
but her face, what she feels, what's between us
are invisible, unknown. Mother,
the tart, oily, blood-loud lipstick you wore
when I was thirteen, in bed, choked with asthma,
and you'd bend to kiss me . . .
I can taste its sour smear now. Last night,
with friends, I told them how I
picked my father's grave, paid for it,
bought the stone, had the ashes put in,
and you still won't go near it.
The man has dragged himself back in.
The woman, inside now, too,
leans over him trapped in his waist-high cast

on the floor, legs propped on a fruit crate,
a miniature TV between his fat white feet:
moon–blue forms squirm over his face, over
the stove and pots, long spoons and glasses,
shift, seem to embody
those final meanings I still seek
in books about God.
She sets the table, puts out a steaming bowl,
near a jar with tall red flowers
spreading from it, she lights a candle.
The man's head follows her. Birds hunch on the branches,
        in the eaves,
and the truth that all I love, all I have touched
will die floods me. *Liar! Liar!*
I hear you, Mother, drunk, screaming on the phone last week.
Lamps, chairs,
each worn familiar object shines.
Wind jolts the branches.
The air halts like a sleeper's breath between our houses.
It's like being a god, seeing this.

No Word

Inside each of us
there's a mammoth dome of light
like the one sheltering me
when I walked out that night
alone in the middle of pines
in Maine, near the ocean.
Black wherever I looked,
even my arms and hands.
I reached out and grabbed a spray of needles,
then tried to see down the path
I knew went in front of me
through elms and brush to water.
Nothing. So I looked up
and found it, flowing in its white fires above my face,
with no word for what it is,
as when a face turns toward you
on the street and you recognize
someone you do not know.

Sketch

This place at the beginning of winter flares
until its last yellow is earth,
and you know what is not yours:
everything, even yourself,
trying to find words, or not.
You step to the window, inside and outside dark,
and lift it to the first brief chill
of far snow. Shapes lurch through the woods,
and their cries threaten as they go.
Dedicated to what there is
of naked vine and leaf, you wait
lost in the silence the word is.

Oblivion

1

I thought the Greek root would tell me something I didn't know
but there is no Greek root – ME, MF, fr. L. oblivion-, oblivio
and then to forget, perhaps fr. ob- *in the way* + *levis*, smooth –
an act or instance of forgetting . . . but I thought it meant something
     like where we go
after death, i.e. "to oblivion," the future of us, the true,
inescapable condition of existence without consciousness,
human consciousness. So it's being forgotten more than anything
that hurts us, and immortality is – to be remembered?
What it really means is what I heard a few months ago
when I said "I've always thought of you as immortal, I guess,
but now I know you're not." and he replied, "Yes, I am. I'm
     in your mind."
It's that "in your mind" that has a kind of murderous tenderness,
it's like saying someone *let* himself be part of you, to help you, yes,
but also because he trusted he could not be destroyed by your mind,
just as a mother takes up a screaming baby into her arms
and croons to it and pats it over and over Now Now Now
     she whispers and presses
the helplessly small body to her breast and it
calms, whimpers, calms fully and falls asleep there.

2

The elephant-gray elms bathed in overcast light glow.
Cobalt blue sky peeps through hills of shaggy clouds.
Windy and cold, 30 on the thermometer outside my window,
chirpings off to my right from behind Jim Wilson's house,
branches stripped clean, bouncing and waving, the day bright,
     brighter,
then darkening under speeding clouds, everything held,
accepted, in an order, the mind and world one

forgetting in which only this moment has meaning. It's much
　　much clearer now.
All's changed color: the lime-freckled salmon brick of Jim's house,
for example, suddenly flares crimson, fists of ailanthus pods
and stuccoed housewalls seem the same bleached tan, even the
　　copper cross
(lived here ten years never noticed it) perched on the church tower
a block northeast is greener, complete because of the light.
But it's the jumble of stacked, rusting
tricycles and two-wheelers leaning against the side of a house
　　on the backyard shed roof
and the oval yellow plastic wading pool tilted on edge
next to them and the cement bucket, white, left on the shed and,
　　most, the homemade red
white and blue doghouse planted a few feet from the shed
that give this life its fullness, for now –
the miniature, peaked, green tarpaper roof and doorless door
　　look kind,
a gift of absent hands, of animals taken in, fed.

From the Bridge

This time it happened as he crossed
the bridge over the defunct
railroad spur behind the warehouse—
Do it Do it—he counted
the rusted tracks, bouquets
of tall weed, fat concrete sockets
for the feet of the silver bridge.
Do it Do it Do it this time
it took that form. He stopped
and cautiously observed all
the things that had been cast there,
shoes, years of paper, bottles,
cans, boxes, car parts, weird shapes.
Which is what we become so why
worry or try to comprehend
anything even that impulse
tolling in his skull, that two-word
delicate command from some
source of revelation and grace
and truth at the core of his mind.
The mind does have a "core,"
where life and death are the same,
where nothing matters, not even
. . . who knows? The day was fairly clear
and not hot, "pleasant" is probably
the word you'd hear if you dialed
the weather, and yet there was nothing
he could do about
the desire of others. *Do it*
was the result of absorbing
that desire, he understood, as he
leaned on the scabby, dented rail,

a desire to have more, to
know what will come next, to
be sure of why and when.
But how can we *have* those?
"When nothing you do will do, what
do you do?" Hisamatsu asks,
and that's about the same as *Do it*,
in a voice not his, not anyone's,
the anonymous possibility
of choosing this. Well, he was walking to
his office, Saturday, to clear up
work, write letters, think,
he was trying to connect his pain
with something that would modify
his relationship to pain,
make it no particular person's,
certainly not his. But all he
knew was the unqualified
numb feeling on the bridge that
to be alive is not better
than to lie with the tracks, waste
metal, paper, and glass
like a thing, and why not, he thought, why not,
after all it *is* someone else,
not me, chanting that puny sentence
Do it Do it like the crowd
at a football game, and it must be
wonderful not to want at all
like junk decaying on cinders
that winks when you move your head.

Gratitude

Sunday. Nothing to do. I park.
Stumps, twigs, crates sail by, gusts wrinkle the water,
blur it, breath on a mirror.
The river's high, the soft banks barely hold it,
sun surfaces and sinks behind haze,
too early for the spectacular pink fire of the cherry,
and in me I hear again Jeff say
"My mother and her mother needed each other so much
they died three weeks apart," in me
my mother cries bitterly for the love she needs
and I'm like a child raging with useless love,
but I listen,
the suffering I brought with me almost gone.
I light a cigar and watch the wrapper blacken.
I think of my mother someday being gone,
of Jeff's father – when we met last, a month before he died,
we discussed the plump strawberries he raised each year
          on his apartment balcony,
the rows of boxes swelling with fruit,
how he loved their tart sweet taste.
One day the first people who loved you are gone –
"unparented helplessness" some fictioneer calls it in a story
about himself as a kid listening to his mother
raging, incapable of love, crazy, dying of cancer,
begging for help, refusing to let him help.
It begins to rain. Driving back,
I scan the brown-green, wavy layers of creased urgent
          slate hillside
glistening five stories high, and Buson's thirteen rocks,
punctuating the infinite, appear,
Stryk's *Awakening*, at dusk
where he is taken into the darkness, joyfully, like the trees,
          "fully aware,"

Lu Yu's old old man running his hands delicately over rocks,
sighing, wondering, "Why can't I make myself stony, like you?"
appear and will always appear.
Wild, truculent geese pass over, honk, hang
on a shelf of wind until it breaks and they veer away.
It rains harder. The windshield blurs and clears.
On the other bank waves claw at steps built into the water,
trees shine, slow lines of cars,
dense, fluorescent red azaleas bush upon bush crowd the road –
each flower has a second one nesting inside –
the birds and rocks gone,
the people gone, the oldest human pain –
not being oneself wholly – gone.

In It

I love being here, like this.
Off to my right, the gold cross of a church,
dumb, tense, symmetrical, there;
soft, late afternoon, pink,
pre-spring Philadelphia light. Beautiful.
I'm in it now, seeing us on the way back
from teaching all day at the university.
March 12th, about 6 o'clock.
Stacks, buildings, wires, billboards, all on the sky,
all the horizon. Driving like this I hear—

inside the bubble of the car,
inside the pure, perceiving, thoughtlessly calm mind—
I know I know it it is there there
You sit next to me, listening,
staring ahead at nothing, everything.
I know that flower of emptiness
when the self touches the world in a deep blur
and the mind opens and is anything;
know, too, the plain, unintrospective sense

of being here: roofing is advertised,
rugs, Toyotas, office furniture; darkness
seeping in turns the sky a vague blood color,
each thing begins to be another,
and, for a time, being human is this.
Air *shhh*, tires *shhh*, the engine
taking us by warehouses, row houses, bleak
hulks and uninviting streets, off-ramps. Lights go on,
inaudibly, sky inky blue. Back there, we saw
grass stubbling the cold, mild fields of Princeton.

Back there, birds undulated in a flock,
black, ominous dots gathering—a shape, a flow—

like indecipherable words that were alive, true.
Now, as we descend the ramp,
I'm with my students in the classroom – they ask,
grimace, doze, read, study the walls, the sky;
empty of this time and place, I'm back –
I love being there with them, talking poetry, seized unexpectedly
by pine boughs caught in a high wind thrashing against the
        windows while Andy
Gratz explains in his casual, clinical way
something difficult in another's poem.

I could sit all day in that seedy room
just listening, butting in, trying to say why
rhythm and meaning *must* be one, etc.
We glide under the immense, blue, concrete-and-steel
footings of the Walt Whitman Bridge, and feel small.
Black and white wavy bars, like zebra hide,
stamp the blacktop. Light through a grating. Here.
Light fuzzy with smoke and time as it grows dark. Back there.
Driving with you asleep, I see
eye-level red clouds scooting across; raw
seeded hills, scallop-topped, sprouting in patches, washed pale brown,
        green, following both sides of the road.
And distance, hazeless after yesterday's hard rain.
I'm in it, as I just said,
and what it is is who I am, and then
the phrase *is there* stuns me and won't go away.
I dip my hand into a half-pound bag
of peanuts I bought with Bob at a store across
from the Writing Program office. We were talking about poetry.
He bought Camels, and said maybe
we'd see each other again soon, maybe
in Philly, where I am now, as

I zip past the bridge and turn right for home,
down Second Street: brooms, ladders, mattresses, stoves
        spotlighted in windows.

He wore an old tan corduroy shirt, sweater, dungarees.
Two different thickness laces in scuffed shoes.
Reg, Ted, Michael, Bob and I
sat in my office discussing prosody.
I grab three or four nuts and crack one
with one hand and steer the wheel with the other, flick off
half the shell and pop two into my mouth and chew.

In the store Bob and I discussed prose, too,
whose truth is desire satisfied immediately
when no meaning lurks behind or deep in it.
Is there anything we can say we know?
It's near dark now; we reach the block-long Greek Revival
        Free Library.
Starlings by the thousands vibrate, as always, below
its grim, official cornices; their lewd,
meaningless twitterings could be a sign. Lawn-lights bathe

the facade, and it reminds me when I was a kid I'd switch on
        a flashlight
under my chin at Halloween to look ugly, scary.
Wide-eyed I'd rehearse in dark in the bathroom mirror.
Small pleasures now; being at one with you.
I think I know where I am, and who; and turn right.
Up the hill. Know. Don't know. Neither. At a lecture last night
the speaker told an anecdote about a poet-friend of his
who felt sure that the woman in a certain Vermeer had finished
        licking her lips just
before the expression she has in the painting. Because of the moisture
you can see glistening – now; because of the strangely unfinished
        closure.

And, hearing that, something joyful about time came clear –
because we want to be so alive, because
we're afraid to be here. Brief, human touches become everything:

light on an eyelid; clean, blond hair; half-consciously whistling
    an old popular tune;
words needed, words received; a warm look –
as I park and scoop up my briefcase and raincoat,
slide out, lock the car, step into my house –
one light dissolves into another,
this 10 x 10 kind of song
talking, making itself free of my tongue.

II

NEW POEMS

Cherries

FOR JEFF

In late April, cherry blossoms engulf the front of the house,
bright bursts, lascivious branches stroking the windows and walls
from a tree the city gave us years ago.
Briefly the petals intensify, soften then fall, and the pavement
one morning is hidden by a dense pink sheet.
I wish I had a mind that could penetrate . . . what? The stubborn
sense of something unrevealed, which might merely be these rooms,
their meals and walls and floors,
their prosaic themes of unstated longing?
At the restaurant last night an old friend
was afraid he wouldn't eat in time to drive back home and see
        his daughters, so he left.
His wife had convinced him to move out, and two agonized
        years later,
starting to live again, he wanted to be in two places at once.
We were sipping wine, talking, watching faces, at home, yet
        I wanted to be
in two places, too, or . . . what is the feeling?
There were sea bass, pompano, trout, on ice,
three tight rows facing us on the counter where we sat
waiting for a table.
They had a freshness I envied, they looked simple,
their scales and harmlessness, sleek oval shapes and motionless
        poise, empty eyes, locked mouths, calm.
"Is my understanding only blindness to my own lack of
        understanding?"
But there is no understanding today, only wanting . . . what?
The tree is stripped; its translucent leaves tint the air.
Our entire pavement and front steps are glutted with petals.
My friend calls to tell me
he finds no solace because his wife still haunts him,

and I say we all have a version of this,
this other, nameless sector of the mind, where
we can only partly live.
We call the petals beautiful, miraculous, a gift, as if they marked
        the path to that something just out of reach,
but aren't they so truly what we are it's a threat —
soft, faded, blown off when the time comes, trampled,
        without desire?
The light's gray this morning.
Even the pavement's cunning veil of seduction, its praise of sorrow,
        can't console.

Writing Class

The student all the way down
at the end of the long table said –
"If you were *my* father you'd
drive me crazy." "Why?" I thought
to myself, what have I done
to her to . . . oh, well. Then
I left the room to copy
a Lowell essay on freedom
in poetry while the students wrote
and on the way back
remembered the story
about her cop father's pink
Harley, and about how much
she loved him. But something else
kept coming into my mind,
though I still can't find the words –
Isn't it strange how we resent
or fear another's mind sometimes?
It's like hating the weather
because it's cold or glary,
or like not having money,
enough to buy a dress you want
or an expensive suit –
maybe why he chose pink
and how it feels to ride the thing
wide open without one thought
was the "something else." We sit
thirty feet apart. We write.
The table's cluttered with white sheets.
Head down, I hear

ballpoints rolling against wood,
maybe even a faint roar
from her old man's hot exhaust,
surely its bleak equivalent
all alone all alone

Sticks

Despair was what I called
what drove me into my yard
to prove my love of nature, to clean up
winter debris – sticks mostly –
if I pushed my nose near leaves, if I bent down
astonished by detail: veins, cracks and lucent pools
trapped in the folds of rock, green stems, moss clumped
        on bricks,
first leaves the size of a baby's fingernail
popping out of every branch I came on
maybe I'd live forever.
A Little Sally Raisin Creme Pie wrapper
had caught in the leaf tangle
of grapevines planted between us and our neighbor,
its dirty cellophane
note from no one to nobody nowhere.
That usually happens when I go out to commune.
I'll be hoping for the cosmic philosophical
and what I'll get is a fuck symbol –
a smiling teen piece in a short skirt,
cunt whiffs of wet earth, moist
shiny bushes that have flourished overnight.
But I gathered leaves, stray
foam nuggets used to pad things in shipping,
plus, fallen dead from the trees, various sticks
which I clipped and made into two neat piles.
In the chilly morning sun
their twin forms
glowed with oriental mystery.
By that time I had worked up a hard-on
and held Little Sally's mouth on it for at least an hour
until, back inside, all I had to do
was lift her perfect body on to me.

Prayer

Nobody understands so let the Rabbi
mutter his texts advise tell us how life should be
let the cantor wail open us
his jagged voice inconsolable praise

I took my mother's face into my hands and kissed her face
       and put my face
against her face and pressed my face against her face her tears
       my tears
and kept my face against her face listened in the dark hospital room
"My mother never held me I never told anyone . . . this . . . "

"How we manage to live so much in the trivial emotion of the daily
when we know what's really important lurks there waiting for us,
and, always, one way or another, finds us," wrote my friend Charlie
and Chekhov's "The soul of another lies in darkness . . . "

I quote these here to console

Lament

My mother wants to be burned, she told me
last night stretched out watching TV
after I told her what the doctor said.
"Don't put me anywhere, either," she added.
I left the room, came back
and found her leaning out a window,
fondling, whispering to the slick branches
of the cherry tree, freshly budded,
shiny after rain,
that brushed the front of my house,
pulling them against her naked breasts
to soothe herself with the cool leafy wood,
to feel something other than her own hands
touch the nipples.

Rubber Rats

You know what it's like Sundays to
wash, brush your teeth, pull on pants and sneakers
then amble to the grocery a few blocks away
for juice, milk, bagels, carry them back,
make coffee, toast – you know it. But the box of rats
brimming onto the counter as I left seemed
all wrong, vile, what's the word?, with its ad
of black wild rats, fangs bared,
lunging in cartoon speed lines at babies,
blood spurting from soft thin white thighs.
The box looks as full this weekend as it did the last,
the heaped-up bony playthings haven't been sold.
They gleam like a contained plague
seething in our sleep, which they did
in mine this week although I didn't actually see one.
Instead, a lovely unidentifiable woman in a blue silk sheath,
stained near the neck, lifted it slowly over her head
and showed her gorgeous naked rat-bitten body, motherly,
        not girlish,
and waited for me on the verge of a smile, in this dream.
What deaths we create for others, what mirrors of denial.
Or what? How much of me is a rat free in the streets
urged on by the blessing of hunger or sick love,
and who was the person who offered herself,
yes, no question, out of kindness,
and what else?

Shoeshine

I asked my ailing mother if she beat me,
if she ever screamed at me for doing things wrong
or wouldn't let me go out to play
because of her fears.
I was trying to know why I feel terror
from a skin bump, a shift in the weather,
a sick look in a passing stranger's eyes.
She said, "I always polished your shoes each night
But I never punished you if you got them dirty the next day."
"No, that's not it, Jesus," I moaned,
"did you ever... were you strict, harsh, cruel, you know..."
"Well, if you threw rocks at people I'd give you a verbal lashing...
look this isn't going anywhere, you won't get the answers here."
And we changed the subject.
Those shoes, taken and put back while I slept,
still glimmer in darkness,
their deep sheen vibrates with the promise of first light.
What can little black, brown or white shoes immaculate
no matter what shit they picked up during the day mean now
again and again resurrected
like mock replicas of the abyss
yawning precisely where my feet would be
when I woke and swung them down?

Through Glass

Nothing below me moves except a fan blade,
starting and stopping on the roof, and one
fat pigeon wobbling across bright tar.
"can't stop hoping" "the next person you meet"
"face the harsh" "spiritual"
ooze their blank lubricious music of 1991,
each time a different meaning, different tone.
Bricks. Patches of weak sky.
Gunmetal clouds foam out from behind a cornice.
Queasy nothingness shapes caught in windows
flash, squirm.
Wonderful distant mirrors of no mind,
go fuck yourselves, go fuck your absent answers.
Flesh questioning flesh,
I've spent all day doing nothing
until questions and flesh are one
bearable breath. . . .
                    A man
yesterday when I was rushing to the gym
appeared, pushing an old wheelchair:
a thick white towel padded the canvas seat,
a pair of shiny black calfskin wingtips,
toes forward, laces tied, sat in the middle of it.

Bandage

My mother acted like a god, crazy, because grown-ups are crazy,
and sat there banging the piano non-stop while my father and
      his mistress
jibbered about their love, she kept playing wildly
through their words. I must have been somewhere, but this
      came to me
only as a story so I'm embellishing, filling out a sketch
I try to see her, two long strong hands flitting across keys
      almost an hour,
my father and his girl side by side on card chairs
explaining, their lips working in the stunned silence of my
      distance, then, now,
a Van Gogh sunflowers on one wall, a Cezanne landscape on another.
Where was I, why was I always out of sight
when terrible things happened? What was she playing? Popular?
      Classical?
Where was my little dog? What was the weather? What meanings
      stung the air?
How did my mother's face look when I burst in finally out of
      nowhere?
There is something very wrong with this world of people.
Maybe you can tell me what it is, if you agree, maybe you
have had such queer pain all your life, squirming in you like a
      hot wire,
and can't find speech for it either and believe you never will, believe
a blinding innocence was forced upon you as if they bandaged
      your eyes —
sent you out to play or buy milk to "spare" you while they did it —
so they could place it, right there, inside you
next to the elegant thick gold petals and bluegreen hills of the
      Dutch and French.

Unfinished Double Sonnet

"Life is forever turning toward a man an infinitely vacant,
      discouraging, hopeless, blank side
on which nothing is written . . ." or
" . . . I always think that the best way to know God
is to love many things . . . one must love with a lofty
and serious intimate sympathy, with strength, with intelligence,
and one must always try to know deeper, better and more.
That leads to God, that leads to unwavering faith . . ." or
" . . . I think that if one keeps one's serenity and good spirits,
the mood in which one is acts as a great help." Of course. Oh yes. Yes.
Please, Vincent, say more: "You talk of the emptiness you
      feel everywhere . . ."
he wrote Theo – to help, to prove God exists,
to say to his brother: We must see Him, touch Him, believe
that His great wisdom made trees, bridges, fields, skies, ears,
      crows – or
" . . . a splash of black in a sunny landscape . . ."

"A caged bird in spring knows quite well that he might serve
      some end;
he feels well enough that there is something for him to do,
but he cannot do it . . ." "One cannot always tell what it is
that keeps us shut in, confines us, seems to bury us, but still
one feels certain barriers, certain gates, certain walls . . ." "Do you
      know what frees one from this captivity? It is very deep
      serious affection. Being friends, being brothers, love,
      that is what opens
the prison by supreme power, by some magic force. But
      without this
one remains in prison." Please, Vincent, say more:
"What am I in the eyes of most people? . . . a disagreeable man . . . the
lowest of the low. Very well . . . then I should want to show

by my work what there is in the heart of such an eccentric man,
of such a nobody" ". . . a Robinson Crusoe or anchorite . . .
      otherwise one has no root in oneself, and one must never
      let the fire go out of
one's soul, but keep it burning."
Oh yes. Yes. What color is the soul?
. . . a splash of black in a sunny landscape . . ."?
". . . the mysterious brightness of a pale star in the infinite."?

from

SHAVING

(a work in progress)

Iowa

When I think of it now I still see just how ugly and dirty the place was, just what a bare unprotected monk-like life it was that year, living first in the old tire warehouse on the outskirts of town, no toilet or sink, no furniture, nothing except two ratty mattresses, fruit crates, blankets from home, unfinished splintery lath walls, gobs of oozed gray mortar stuck between the bricks, and everywhere the bitter acid stink of tire rubber, the acrid air of dirt and dust, everywhere in high black stacks truck tires, car tires, hundreds, except for one small room, probably an office once, where we slept and read. The teeth-like treads gleamed in the dark. Some nights I'd choke with asthma from the filth, from rage, from how far away home was. Some nights we'd lie in our room reading by the sallow light of the small bulbs of the bed lamps we got at a junk shop and nailed up on our walls. Outside, the fields of Iowa went on forever, a ditch of yellow mud bordered the north wall. Some nights Bob and I would bundle up in everything we owned and go out and stare at the shoals of stars, pale surfy light-blotches pulsing slightly, go out half-drunk and stand in the lampless cityless darkness rambling about poetry, family, sex, loneliness, about almost anything. Once, I remember, I took out an old silver Bach cornet I had picked up in a pawnshop in town for 15 bucks and tried to play the thing, stood on the edge of the ditch leaning back and pointing the horn straight at the sky, but all that came were a few squawky mewing fart-like tuneless wails, jagged held notes, and at one point – the horn against my lips – I took a wrong step into the ice-crusted watery slough and stumbled and fell and almost broke off my front teeth. For months I carried the mouthpiece in my pocket, fondling it, taking it out to heft, practicing on it to build my lip, *fweeting* a few raw notes when I felt like it – walking across campus, on the street, anywhere. I kept myself company like that, I became somebody else, mostly Bix, because I envied his sweet pure tone, the steadiness and range, his quick, condensed phrasing, the direct brevity of his style, a miraculously articulated, clear, triumphant sadness. But before long we took an apartment in the heart of town – had cleaner mattresses, desks, a couple of chairs, bookcases built with cinder blocks and boards – two rooms, a big double door between them, where we'd each write, often at the same time early in the morning or late at night. It was wonderful being serious about writing, seeing oneself as capable as the stars of moving someone, of holding a human gaze, wonderful feeling haunted, if you were lucky, by lines, impulses, hot unformed combinations of phrases that led your hands over the keys at a speed beyond understanding, beyond experience. Then out would come the paper with words on it and you'd begin again – chop, change, shift, hack, put something back or stick it somewhere else, anything seemed possible in that mood – to hear the necessary mind of the poem. Otherwise it was classes and the usual college shit: football games, parties, gossip, worry about grades. Then the snow came and everything was lost under it, everything slowed. Sometimes it fell hip-deep. People wallowing through it would plow paths along the sidewalks and across the streets at corners. The quads and fields were cratered and scarred with ruts like a moon map glowing blue-white. It's hard to give you the mood of Iowa City after one of those big snows but I was happier then than I knew, trapped there, purified of choice by isolation, schedules breaking down, the roads out of town impassable for a day or two. We'd stay up till three or four in the morning, playing pinball machines in an all-night diner a few blocks away, or reading and trying to write. The vividness of words on a page in a book, the sound of the human voice on a printed page was never more compelling and intense than on those long nights of immense peaceful silence while the snow under the street lamps simply lay there, consolingly white and quiet, going on for miles. The Workshop Quonsets looked like sleeping animals, down by the Iowa River. You could walk across it and not step through; you could see, you believed, the wide gray street of water underneath roiling past. It made my scalp prickle to see the uncountable rows of footprints crossing and recrossing ("lovely wounds in the snow"), blurred intersected patches embellishing the snow-riddled lid of ice. It looked eerie, too meaningful – why, I still can't figure out – the bright, pocked, luminous crust scored by those shadowy all-alike holes. And nothing came there, not at night in the bleak Midwestern cold, unless an animal happened by. The still, dry cold drove people together, inside. But that was only one thing it was good for. By day or at night, if you were out of town (after the roads were plowed) where it begins to seem nothing exists but fields, endless open fields, if you looked across the sugary land, blindingly flat by day, serene and muted at night, you might say that the silence and the peace you felt had always been and always would be; even the three black wires overhead threading out of sight in both directions couldn't disturb that belief; you might also come to see that the simple two-lane road and the spare sharp gray houses, silos, barns and little scattered buildings had been placed there by people who do not care where they live so long as it rests in the midst of such deep quiet – farms cleanly fenced to hold animals and mark property lines, so far from many people, so far from needing you. And another thing that sticks with me I can't quite shape with words was one night borrowing a girl's red Jaguar four-door sedan, belting down a few then leaving town to pick up the interstate, rifling away, and, aware I was feeling nothing, aiming down the endless chute at the point where houses and trees stop and almost nothing is left but the road and dark, and a few faint shapes, a few houselights are visible, just there where the world seems to peter out, slapping down my foot on the gas pedal, flooring it, keeping it there until I was absolutely sure I was alive, still alive, seeing the long white shining walls spit from the snowplow, risen on each side of the road higher than the car, rush by, go through me into infinity.

Talking

If you knew where suffering comes from, if you could fathom that one last fraction of its source, the root tip that seems unreachable, mystical, wouldn't you starve just to see it, talk to it, hold it between your hands, shield it, let it be heard, isn't it the one thing you'd rather know than anything – where the dread comes from when it seeps into your belly and chest, into you, like a stink you hit driving the turnpike – skunk, pig shit, chemicals – or like one's poor conscience crying No! No! You can't do that, can't say that. You believe the "you" you are might even disappear if you act, speak, begin to reveal what's there, wherever "there" is, whatever "it" is that wants and does not want to be heard. Some still call it the soul but it's what we know about ourselves that's still inside us, what Sartre calls the "depth of darkness" in us. Some mornings you get up needing to share the "dark region" that can "only be illuminated for ourselves in trying to illuminate it for others." You sit at your desk, sip coffee: images, traces of comprehension, words evaporate: you flip through books in stacks already gnawed at, underlined, page after page, look out the window, flip through books – "A man's existence must be entirely visible to his neighbor, whose own existence must be entirely visible in turn, before true social harmony can be established." You type – background of birds and traffic – and look outside again as the voices inside you you wish would speak fade and go silent. Titles on spines. Page edges. "When once the truth is grasped that one's own personality is only a ridiculous and aimless masquerade of something hopelessly unknown, the attainment of serenity is not very far off," Conrad says in one of his letters on life and art. In Princeton once, I drifted through the library into the rare books wing and saw all of his books, first editions, standing on edge or propped on wire easels, some closed flat on their backs in glass cases or lined up on shelves, some spread open with ribbon to the frontispiece – his prissy Vandyke beard and narrow sorrowful puzzled black eyes stare, a high collar, white, propping up his chin, his suit jackets buttoned to the last, top button, almost to the neck. What an incongruous formal figure he cuts in those photos and lithos when you think of the pain in his books, his relentlessly etched landscapes, his disheveled tortured men being peeled away until they see themselves and are left in the abyss of mind, of self, of nature, suspicion worming out their brains, all substance charred in the fires of moral possibility, a maze-like gloom suffusing the world. "... the rescued fragment..." is a phrase from one of his essays that haunts me. "The task approached in tenderness and faith is to hold up unquestionably, without choice and without fear, the rescued fragment before all eyes in the light of a sincere mood." Or Stein to Marlowe: "How to be!... We want to in so many ways to be." Or "... another man's infinite need..." and what it is "... to grapple with it." "Needed rather than needing" my old friend Charlie calls it in a letter to me: "One night at Tex's, while I was waiting for Catherine to come out of the bathroom so I could start the porno movie, I was flipping the channels and came to a broadcast of the Hasid Convention in New York, some big special thing when the Hasids from all over the world come to hear the head Rabbi speak. I was stoned, sort of drifting, watching it, they were all from some other epoch, bearded, hats, chanting something, and there was a voice-over that must have been translating the Rabbi's sermon or something, and it said something that really struck me, something, I don't remember in what context, human or divine, but I took it to mean human, about being needed rather than needing..." Charlie wrote that after an hour we spent on the phone listening to each other probe anguishes to the point where each of us heard the other the way a mother goes to its infant's cry and lays her face against its face in love that needs nothing for itself, that has no self, that hears the very center of the child's anguish so it knows and can sleep. The muted tenderness in every copy of Conrad's face, the dignity in his fear of love, the heavy-lidded oriental eyes and thin mouth felt alive. He and I were alone in the big silent room. Some of the books showed a page he had dedicated or signed.

One case held six full-face portraits, all with the stiff high collar crowding his chin, dark jacket buttoned to the top, nothing suggesting jungle, ships or oceans. I kept strolling around, stopping, looking, reading whenever I saw a page of text or a letter. In not one etching or photo does he look straight ahead out at the reader so you'd feel he is looking *at* you, his eyes stray off to the left or right, half-shut, scouring blank distance that goes on and on, poised, waiting to hear someone, you, perhaps, speak and expect an answer, speak in the fullness of his need.

The Coat

FOR JERRY

Here's one of those warm simple letters in that big six-year-old scrawl of yours, filling the whole page with your statement, clear, sweet, kind, associating values with detail with Nietzsche with the glory of poetry with some local flower or creature you bumped into yesterday and fell in love with, with the rich tweed coat I gave you last time you were here. "Jews understand coats, life-giving coats, protection against death," you say in the letter, and "It's easy being crazy when the house is empty, thinking of birds of prey wearing black hats." Jerry, the yellow Irish raglan-shoulder coat I bought with money from my father is yours now, it's draped on your beefy Hebrew shoulders in the sticks near Easton, Pa., where nobody has good taste, nobody will admire its nubby random unassuming weave, its hand-loomed itchy grain brimming with dots of pink. Where you live it's as if cities don't exist yet, all's primitive, all's survival. Your neighbors pace the canal near your house, naming weeds, studying the water level, diagnosing soil richness, filling plastic sandwich bags with specimens: butterflies, quavering nameless insects, leaves, semi-precious stones. But none of them know shit about coats, their cloudy bone buttons and waxed thread sewn crisscross over and over until there's a sharp lump the owner can rub his thumb across for comfort. It's a Burberry, you schmuck, and you probably couldn't care less. It didn't fit from the day I picked it out, its long tent-like form comes from the past of animal pelts and capes and blankets with a slit cut in the middle, for living in nature not the city where people love clothes that "enhance" the body. Russians know coats, don't they? and Jews, those death-fearing, Godless, touchy maniacs of the world who need their vulnerable, paranoid bodies, ecstatic, wrapped in a heavy expensive coat – so gas fumes can't penetrate, so torture can't swell their ankles and wrists, so the ideas of clean rigid Gentiles who believe in social justice, in eliminating obstructions to justice, can't get in, so the hands of strangers on a bus or in a street crowd can't reach their delicate skin, so even the hands of tender love can't change their mood. Eliot, Pound and Joyce bought themselves coats, showed off gorgeous Isle of Skyes, Meltons, sheared camel hairs, hoping it would drop below zero just to test how absolute their coats were, whether they were true mortal coats that could give life, define life, save life. What a Jewish idea! But I believe it. A coat so well-made, so thick and fine it could actually prevent death: an immortality coat! Right now I want my coat back, Jerry, even though it's late May, it's the only coat I know that might help me live forever, but I give myself a stupid effeminate kiss in the long bathroom mirror instead, down to my crotch, I begin to lather and shave, a kiss instead of a coat, and feel the just sadness of how much I'll miss that sack of stitched woven hair come December. Naked, I shave, an hour before leaving to teach, zipping the blue plastic Good News across cheek over chin up to the lip under a nostril and it strikes me that I should lecture on coats today not poetry, inspired by the coat I gave you, which has probably fallen off its cheap wire hanger by now, a blurred heap among gashed rubber boots, the vacuum cleaner, outgrown ice skates, dark twisted hats and whatever else you've chucked down there to be sold at a yard sale. My lecture should explain the coat's power to stop death and somehow should, I think, represent divine coats in an act that uses a real coat somehow. I'll wear one of my coats to class. I walk in. Take out my note cards, still wearing my coat. I keep it on. Suddenly they're quiet. I'm talking about the coat, your coat, the coats. Brilliant. Euphoric. Letting my mind speak, wandering in all its honest blindness. And I add "Lusting for a hundred things this morning, I'd rather have a coat than anything, deep, unassailable wool to shield a back and chest on a cold night so securely that the man who wears it feels he can stand anything, do anything, survive even his own death, grateful for the feel of it, for the weight, for the reassuring dense goodness against his bare hands, for the shiny trace of oil it leaves in a film on his palms and fingers." Then I call one student up and draw her inside my

180

coat by opening it like Dracula, still lecturing, and button us in and feel her jump when my crazy stiff dick springs and pulses against her belly, still lecturing about coats, whispering, declaiming, gesturing, making scholarly digressions, invoking history, origins, fashion, cloth, hissing out of the side of my mouth to her—"Stay calm, don't let anybody know," as her hand slips it in a little and I sway a little, finishing, asking questions, answering questions, blithely in touch with their faces as she comes, three or four muffled tremors, all this time both our faces turned toward the class, and she's tittering as if the whole thing is merely a lecture on coats. "What a beautiful coat you have," she says, "so roomy, warm," and I thank her for the compliment, say "But you should see the one I gave Jerry," unable to recall one thing I've said to the class during the last few minutes. Ah, this life, which even the best coat can't protect us from; this death, too strong for the warmest coat there is. Nevertheless, there are coats that will never let us die—I know it. Every time I step into the hall closet and sniff its musty dark and rove my hands over the coats—first shoulders, then the long drape of the body—awed by their dark softness, and caress mine, I pray it's one of those coats, the holy ones, I close the door and stay in there as long as I can, blindly nuzzling and singing.

Brothers

All through childhood I never could quite find a place in my family where I fit, at least that's how it feels to me now when I try to see what it was like in our house – a grandfather dying of heart disease, grandmother, mother and father, no brothers or sisters – what it was like to be my mother's obsession. It isn't that I can say what act, habit or word hurt me, exactly: I was who I was only through her eyes. Her overprotective, phobic love stunned me with fear. My rowhouse was an only child's cocoon that hummed with argument or silence. I can't find myself at the table with family, at a movie with grown-ups. So few clear details substantiate my time there, I can't believe I ate, talked, slept, was a son, a little boy wishboning his pet terrier's hind legs until she'd yelp. I'd see a baby in a carriage and hate it, but I couldn't see my own new, mutilated soul and stop myself. I do see one terrifying dawn when I was five and had just waked: I lifted my head off the pillow and looked past my feet where a huge blue human torso, no face, no fingers, legs or hair hung in the window for a minute like a clump of mist, evaporated and left me shaken. What did it mean? Who was I except someone others saw? But that's not the real story. Looking back, everything's either baseball with other kids, scooping ice daggers like glass arrowheads off the back of the truck and sucking them, step ball, sledding; everything's outside, in the street, a vacant lot, an alley, except for a few bare images soaked in the gloom of home. With friends I fit, with them I could do anything, I believed, and not be watched and judged, not be the boy whose life his mother feared for. The one I remember best today had had polio and walked with a stiff limp, his right leg seemed to be locked or frozen straight, his right arm hung perpetually bent now and the hand had that curl-claw affliction that made flipping pages or picking up small things or shaking hands nearly impossible. But he seemed to have been sweetened by the disease, by his parents' tolerance and love. When they were there you could sense the depth of their love – hovering, light smiles glued on their faces, bent forward a bit in an always eager readiness to help, to serve, to replace what that sick twist of fate had damaged with toy after expensive toy, games, athletic equipment, records, books, even a commercial pinball machine that stood plugged in all day and all night (he told me) in a corner of his bedroom, its waiting, glowing, glassed-in field of slots and tinted bumpers, its scoreboard splashed with monsters, war scenes, planes and tanks, invectives branding the red air between the creatures, spewed from their mouths, all as if sent up from some hellish abyss. It stood there like a sentinel guarding the gates to another life, a life I had no inkling of, beneath this life, always beneath this life, a life later I wanted and feared, the place in the mind where truth was. A huge toybox in his room was always open when I visited; it over-flowed into a surf of gameboxes, trains, erector struts, gun bar-rels, softballs, gloves. Metal twinkles drifted everywhere among the rest of that rich jumble like stars in a little homemade sky which opened my mind, as the machine did, but to a life I think I associated with the word Heaven then. What still un-settles me is my first clear flicker of conscience: every time he left me alone in that room of his I'd pick out a small toy I'd been coveting and pocket it or stuff it into my schoolbag. I can't re-member his name. I think he knew I was stealing from him, but it must have been worth it to him just to have someone his age drop in once or twice a week. His skinny, tall, stooped-over, humble kindness, his delight at my arrivals, his calm surrender of desire or will, at his age no doubt inculcated by suffering, saves me today. He walked the way my grandfather did, whose stilted teetering gait as he came toward you across a room made you feel he might fall against you as, inches away, he finally reached you. But about the boy: my mother knew his mother and I was ordered to visit him, play with him at least once a week, he rarely went outside, be nice to him, be good, just as I told myself eight years ago to pick my father's plot and buy the stone and have the border sanded on it and the dates carved in, and pay it off, on time, without help. Is my childhood friend alive? What has his life been like? Does he wear one of those braces where you see the flat shiny chrome strut jut out of the pants leg past the ankle to the arch of the shoe where it meets a rod going across to the inside of the foot, like a stirrup, and attaches to another strut? I can't remember anything we said, but I keep seeing that knowing sincere smile he had, whenever I'd buzz his door and he opened it. I keep seeing myself filching a yo-yo, top or pimple ball. No more than two or three. Really. Then I abandoned him, never went back. Who wants someone who's crippled, has to stay home all day, has to be taken care of. God, what it is to be young, so young that consciousness is barely born. Back then all needs are yours; then, all you're strong enough to know is you, a you that barely exists. But I needed someone to forgive me–for what, I'm still not sure–and he did. After all, kids know when a toy is missing, even when they have more than they need. And look, his tenderness returns just now, he leans above me like a saint, waiting, as my hand searches his toys– both of us invisible, souls, in another world, –his warm hurt eyes accept me: a gaze that says gratitude for friendship is easy, no matter what its terms, his hatred and pity seeing me walk in and walk out on two strong legs would touch me like a brother.

Self-Portrait at Six

My wife hung it there, on the wall on the way to our bedroom. When you take the five steps up to the landing in front of our door, it's on your left, usually in shadow in a gold-rimmed, oval mat, Victorian oval walnut molding frame, the eyes already hurt, defensive in the way we think "open" means but is, actually, only a form of wariness. No steadiness, no self-assurance, no clarity of mind influence the face yet. The thick brown hair is mine, but the mouth is all wonder in a kind of sullen trance and pleads not to be wounded more. He fears the world can kill him, and will, the world is always mysterious, like disease. Being alone attacks him from the outside, saddening his look, he can't ignore it by simply playing. Instead it seems he can't defend himself, there's no courage of acceptance in his gaze. At my age now, I've come to imagine my mother, at the beginning of my life, as a young lovely woman, baffled by her pain, who found my helplessness too much like her own to let her simply reflect my emerging self. So, to extend the thought, my face on the stairwall, then, was already trapped in the battles of identity and self-denial, of believing that freedom is impossible because another feels nearly like who one is. Isn't that what our first taste of death is – invasion of another's pain? Isn't that how we first split ourselves into good and bad? Think of an awareness that lets you act without even a shade of sensing others are watching you, judging you, caring about you, so that desire and action fuse, and there's no gap, no hint of pain that slows you. But this is memory, interpretation, the two great dangers of the mind. What it is I'm getting at, what it is that brings that picture back and stirs my ideas is the gnawing aloneness of people, of all things, of consciousness itself, and the opposite – that each of us lives in others' minds, as they live in ours, sometimes flaring in images, sometimes engrossed in each others' flesh. Each night before I go to bed I pass myself on the stairs, eternally helpless, caught with an early madness crossing my face, and it seems, as I tuck myself in, trying not to be seen or heard, that the entire universe is the dark fetal mound breathing on one side of our bed, that everything flows from it, everything returns.

Behind Us

Those glum, blank-faced, two-, three-story rowhouses in Phil-
ly on the fringes of slums in starved light, glare, look as if layers
of hope have been peeled off, nearly to the bone, a soreness con-
stant as air hurts everything from dogs to storefronts to the tilt,
sag and precarious mortar of old walls and chimneys. Another
layer off and the lath would show. Even in summer a chill reeks
from unknown sources, existence is a cracked plate glass win-
dow, the hardness of an oak school desk chair, a door lock held
on by a single screw, a man leaning against a chain link parking
lot fence, pushing his cheek against the thick cold squares of
wire for comfort. He has on a tan poplin jacket and oilstained
khakis and work shoes spattered with white dust from a build-
ing site. An inch-thick circle of black sock shows. What's life in-
side those rooms, soup spoiling the air with fat, everyone al-
ways almost touching, touching, always hearing each other, TV
snoring away, emanating its trustful gray glow? It took at least
an hour, riding through that neighborhood, on the street be-
tween slum and near-slum, to reach the bike shop in Chestnut
Hill, its main street jammed with Shoppes, colonial facades in
yellow, putty and blue, their windows crammed with cheeses,
garden tools, skis, crystal, imported wool, the cobbled streets as
clean as country roads – a WASP paradise. Millie and I were
going to the Hill Cycle Shop to pick out our daughter's Christ-
mas gift, a 10-speed bike. We chatted on the way, watched
people stepping off, and on, marvelled at how far over on a
curve the trolley would lean and not topple, at the crookedness
of the track that would jerk the car and clack it to one side then
pop it back straight as it wobbled on its route uphill through
dilapidated shopping districts – black, Irish, Polish – past hand-
made cardboard signs and cars with For Sale signs and a phone
number taped on, old clothes and furniture, spackling in cracks
and blob-shaped patches chipped off, a world used so hard and
long nobody ever had time to stop, to let it rest, to fix or refur-

bish. At one point along the way two fat white wives of blue-collar workers got on and sat behind us, their hair was dyed pale blue oyster white, cut short, curled, sprayed stiff as cocoons. Their skin shone like a bar of margarine, a clean scent flared from them, indistinct, vapid, renunciatory, sweet, the smell that hits you while you browse through a dime store. For blocks there was silence, the monotony of watching obsolete bare stores – a wing chair stuck in a window, a checked wrinkled summer jacket flung down, a faded sleeve, salt and pepper shakers, ashtrays, one with a chrome-dipped naked nymph, arms up, perched on the edge – things drifted to the edge of existence, futility in things. A tall skinny black kid bops up the steps into the car, stands, ass tilted against a pole, one of those massive plastic and chrome ghetto-blasters slung on his shoulder, all three speakers blaring. A few blocks later the doors flap apart and he slips off into the street and I hear one of the women behind us telling her friend a story in a low voice. Fragments of it reach me: "I don't know why . . . my niece Kathy killed herself with pills . . . there's a clinic around the corner from me and I decided to go there, get a doctor, something was scaring me after Kathy, and I'm sitting in his office, I guess it's the third visit, just him and me, and he asks me about my sex life, do you believe it? So I blasted him, I said, 'I'll be god-damned if I'll tell a complete stranger about something like that . . . ' and walked out and never went back." Her niece – all that promise, all that lust of excitement and touch, of being entered and held, youth blowing loneliness away, intimacy, orgasm, the first taste of what makes us want to live, the holiness of pleasure – it must have been a sacrilege for a member of that family, its morality strict as a stoplight, to suicide. It must have been a crime to hear someone connect the death with sex. Then silence. And now, brooding on silence, on a lost unfulfilled soul, on puberty, on poverty's unhealing wound, which, as some say, may be the soul's misunderstood condition of openness to the actuality of soul, I know we can't own anything, we don't and can't, depend on anything, believe in anything, escape anything. Millie and I glanced at each other but we didn't speak. The two women said nothing either after that one tirade or after she blurted her meager worrisome details, clues to the whole tale. Often that's where I am: in the silence of the unexplained that falls after someone's revealed heartfelt killing facts connected to the unspeakable, to unlived life, so an entire family's invisible conections seem suddenly to pluck the air and hum, piercing, unclear, and you feel the struggle to understand and speak to the person who spoke in the seat behind you, because maybe that would offer hope. What can a stranger give to a stranger? A story of his own, one of those incidents of love, lost love, the unending quest to define love? Maybe I should have gotten up and taken the seat behind them – it was empty – and leaned close to their heads and whispered a consolation, anything, what a father might say to his daughter who's come to him and sits in silence, one evening, full of complaint, afraid to discuss the facts behind her pain. "Listen," I might have said, leaning close, "I know what you mean. There's a part of life I never seem able to live, or can't live as fully as I need to, it's hard to explain, but when someone suffers and tells you about it it's as if that part of me I can't make live might die forever in the other person's pain right then... aren't we all looking for the love that helps us to enter... 'this dark region within ourselves, which is at once dark for us and dark for others and can only be illuminated for our selves in trying to illuminate it for others'... you see, the thing is, all this searching, wondering, it doesn't get you out of your life, you're always in your life, and it is true, the idea I have, that we're so mortal God can put His hand through us as if we were air, speaking air, poor fleshless images suspended in air." We reach our stop, still silent, get off, walk a bit, find the bike shop window. The noon sun arches behind us. I press my face to the cold, clean glass – inside out, outside in – listening as the glass listens. No need to speak. Trucks, voices, scufflings buzz on the window, against my face. I move my head back, about an inch, our two transparent faces, the stable world behind us in the street, there, bodiless, as they were before they were, and as they will be, the self-erasing, world-erasing light bathing us the way a mother will dip her infant, gently, bit by bit, into its warm bath.

Music

Behind us, the blank world; in front of us, what we see – buildings, streets, intricate green trees, distance, tattered clouds, a glimpse of brilliant water, her, him, it – always the pure clear absence of God. We stand between, almost like mirrors facing mirrors, and "almost" is the key: we're almost here. "We are lost in childhood," Sartre moans, and I believe it, but I'm not sure what it means. Rimbaud stopped writing poetry when his puberty faded at eighteen on the edge of madness, then chose the world of business, where intelligent song doesn't mean shit, where the words "visionary" and "apocalyptic" make people laugh, where speech isn't risked to explore mind until words pierce into the lost layer of community, of the need to commune, though that's where the illuminations in his new poems took him. He wears a belt of gold dust and the weight of it causes sores and chafes his organs until they bleed. That's the main fact for me – how he converted poetry into gold, about $40,000.00 worth lugged through jungle and desert until a tumor of the knee stops him and he's taken by litter to Harar, then Roche, Paris, Marseille, too late to save his life. From his diary: ". . . stretched out, with my leg bandaged, tied, retied, changed, in such a way that I cannot move it. I've become a skeleton: I'm an object of fear. My back is all sore from the bed; I can't sleep a minute and it has grown terribly hot here. . . . The litter is already half dislocated and the people completely done in. I try to mount a mule, with my sick leg tied to the neck; I have to get off after a few minutes and return to the litter, which is already a kilometer behind. Arrived at Balawa. It's raining. Furious wind all night." Then of course there's the eerie early Carjat photo of him. Wispy, fuming with adolescent disgust and girlish disdain, already adept at "the sterility of genius," at wasting one life and starting another, he peers off into space from a sorrow that says we have no right to be here, as we are, not conscious enough of our fate, of our debt to the cosmos, trapped in civilization's blind lust for the factory, for goods, for the machine, for the destruction of life lived in "the key of love." One feels at times, listening to his storms of vatic song – pain laminating pain into one premonitory wail – that his hatred and tenderness, his ache to annihilate and save the world clash in permanent simultaneous splendor, that they occur with such force because he realizes desire never can find what it needs, it goes on burning as an inner hell forever, like the sick leg that killed him, like the universe itself. "La musique savant manque à notre désire," he announces in L'Illuminations: No music can fully reveal who and how we are, our infinite shifting selves and faces, our fear of being no one, souls hoping, wishing, craving, probing each other for what has no name as if God placed an invisible veil between each of us, between ourselves and ourselves, between us and Him, that can't be breached or defined though we keep trying to break through – into ourselves, into others – Jesus, what silences we contain. They take his leg at the knee. "Shit to poetry," he screams at one of the doctors, poking his head in to chat. June 23, 1891 four months from death, answering his sister's letter, thanking her, in a way, for the hopeful gift she's sent, (she must not know about his amputation), Jean Nicolas Arthur Rimbaud sums it all up in the pragmatic style that developed once he embraced the kingdom of fact: "The stockings are useless. I will sell them somewhere."

Bread

These people facing me – masons, architects, plumbers, bankers, painters – represent all the trades, professions, businesses, arts, in all these photographs the same uncomplaining, poised, smug look of normalcy, of efficiency masks their faces. It's shameless how they stand there and don't mind being shot head-on, posing for a moment, on the job, distracted from work, a cross-section of Germany. Not a trace shows of the suspicion or the humility or the saddened innocence you see in those who know their weaknesses and are camera-shy. There's something else behind all this – a lurking theme, a revelation. The way they hold themselves you'd think nothing tragic has ever touched their lives: not even the forgotten griefs of infancy or separation or focusing on others. Lust. Friendship. Intimacy. They seem to be glorying in the privilege of simply doing their duty as grown-ups on this simple, justified earth. All soul-disrupting questions, all anguish, all confusion has been smoothed from their knowing faces by the belief in something I can't root out and explain, that haunts me. That's why I'm wandering like this, that's why so far I can only talk *around* what I saw in that Sander show in the museum. It's as if these men and women know they know The Truth so well that now it dwells in the flesh. Maybe the sepia light that gilds each pore of each face, chair, window, tool and wall contains the answer, fire reaching from the bottom up along the walls of a pit, yearning on the faces of the onlookers in an eerie flicker, or a furnace's maw of fuel, banked low, gnawing its orange heart out, spreading its heat. Their expression defies the idea that these clean, stolid citizens might not – materially, spiritually – have everything. Even the low-paid laborer, stopped while widening a ditch, has gratitude in his eyes, and the boy with him, tidying a mound of indescribable debris, milky, stick-like things, leans on his outsized rake blithely detached from the objects of his toil. The fact is I'm imagining this – I remember, mainly, an aura:

ambiguous truce is the mood: I'm sure what I've been "seeing" is based on that, on what these figures project, and I'm caught in that projection the way we live in time and place, always. Politically, I'd guess they existed in transition, exalted by and unaware of it, on the verge of something mammoth, inclusive and insane. Still baffled by their spell, I wish I understood why only one actually comes back, and why a sadness falls when I think of him, taken full-length in front of his shop, reduced so (two feet tall) by photography on the museum wall just above eye-level: me looking at him, him seeming to look at me. He has his apron on. He stands, legs apart. His hair is a foam of dark curls, years younger than his thickening face. His hands, if I remember, are open across his thighs just beneath his crotch and smears of flour and smears of a darkish substance give the stiff cloth texture, depth, grains and patches of contrast. His hands are gloved with flour, as if he has just stepped outside from work, and its shade of white and the white of the cloth and the white skin of his bare huge forearms are very close. A poet could invent some spiritual relationship between them. The whites remind me of bone, an understandable association these days, or of the mind at prayer, but that flour could be anything. We haven't seen him just before this, mixing water and flour, kneading air out of the dough with the heels of his hands, sprinkling flour as he goes, folding the dough back, kneading, squashing out air until the dough is smooth and yields less easily, is dense, less willing to be moved. In the shop windows flanking him, loaves glow. They have been tilted up toward you on racks to display their wounded, seeded, glazed crusts. They look almost like sleeping babies, or like long blank oval faces in the hands of God before He decided who each would be. Their sweet taste is still palpable, old as the photo is, say, 1929. Nearly fifty loaves lying there. Shaped a little like the baker's forearms, they are not white but sandy brown. The tips of the loaves touch the windowglass and shine. The man's moustache covers his whole lip and is trimmed cleanly. His fingernails are square, short and clean. His eyes are passive and don't reveal what I called earlier "something else," "a lurking theme," "a revelation" – what, really, does he hate and tell us the only way he can? What we know and are afraid to say? Flour is beautiful, the perfect symbol of existence, and the idea of flour: that it signifies the fate of the temporary things of temporary earth. When I remember it on his hands, his accepting eyes are mine, horrified, helplessly overtaken as I am now in my time and place. It makes me want to plunge my hands into a drum of cool flour and keep them there sunk up to the wrists for a long, long time and simply stare at the place where the flour and my arms meet. Nevertheless, his mouth: weird: it hangs open at least half an inch, idiotically, brutally, greedily – who knows? – a streak of mucous, gleaming, untranslatably meaningful, starts on his moustache, strings to his lower lip, and the point of his tongue, also bright, like the tip of a finger or of a child's penis, glistens between his teeth.

Lowell: Self-Portrait

When Lowell let me audit his writing course I left New York and rented a furnished room for seven bucks a week on Boston's Revere St. Nothing remains except snow, stray phrases, images fuzzed by awe and time. His class I barely remember. I'm convinced all he did was read our poems aloud, make a few abrupt shy comments after each, flirt, then at the end skulk out fast as if he had committed some private unatoneable crime none of us could possibly consider. One day he doesn't show up. A breakdown, another student tells me, he's in MacLeans again. I call his wife, ask if I can see him and she says fine, he's "only . . . taking a rest." That Friday, about three, I enter Bowditch Hall and ask for him. An attendant leads me to his room – American antique: a bed, rope crisscrossed under the horsehair mattress, burnished orangey desk with a drawer on each side, twin straightbacked spindle chairs, low maple bureau its brass handles aglint in the waning winter sun. I wait, dressed in khaki infantry fatigues, the kind with long flapped pockets on the front of the thighs, pea coat and galoshes. Soon he's there in the doorway, sweating from squash, blue and white striped sailor's jersey, flushed, shockingly healthy; he sits on the bed, facing the windows and the blinding lawns behind me. I sit in a chair, across from him, on the other side of the bed. His small round horn-rimmed glasses brim with white light from the sky and lawns, mirrors almost; my tiny seated figure sits in them, twin color slides; his expressionless powder-blue eyes, faintly visible, seem imbedded in the lenses – it's like seeing myself in another, as another who watches me, a blanked-out false self sick with identity whose instinct is to fix us both into a permanent thing, make seeing and seen sacred, one. It must be I worship him. All I can do is not comprehend, is be there, watch, wonder. He asks me to listen to new poems, from *Life Studies*, reads from the manuscript of drafts stacked in both pulled-out desk drawers, five, six, which poems I can't remember, then asks what I think.

I like the *Lord Weary* poems better, something like that comes out, and he replies (I can hear each wryly pronounced word): "Pound thinks they're either genius or pure shit." What do I know? I turn and look out, taking time to ponder the silence now between us, between the world and us. And all the time the fresh implacable snow turns gray in the early twilight, three rows of alien footprints punch the chaste crust, a few huge tree shadows, blue translucencies, happen, fuse with the dimming heavy fall. Then I look back. A fume of rubbing alcohol blossoms, stings my nostrils, instantly fades. His desk's littered with scrawled-on, neatly typed white sheets, drafts, finished copies, blanks. I glance across the bed into his eyes, held in those eyes. A patient? A saint in a cell? This: the white walls, chalky with glare, scary air between us, dazzle me, I'm not sure who I am or if I'm here, there's nothing inside/outside I can grasp to anchor me, the tangible who-we-are-where-we-are flickers, vanishes, seeps back into the known self. More ragged talk. At day end, side by side, we trudge the drifted long front lawn to the high iron gate in front of the grounds, its black shields and vines trimmed with snowy crests. He stops and I walk on, past the gate; he waves a friendly, fatherly goodbye, keeps waving, sincerely touched by this scared half-boy, I think I can see that on his dwindling face, until the street takes me behind a building out of sight and we go back, naturally, each to his own room. A murmur of crossed voices, one voice; one face no effort can make quite visible; some weird master-disciple incense. Back in my room with the light off, stretched out on the metal cot, I touch, a foot or so away, desk edge, typewriter, vague white paper mess, lean down, switch on the radio on the floor and, dim yellow glow of the dial rimmed with numbers by my face, tune and tune and tune and tune and tune it.

Not That

Some say acceptance is the heart of it, or grief, the "true self" or the here and now, some say it's the "I" behind the infinite ring of selves the "I" really is, but who knows who one is, why and how one is? Sometimes a sentence lets us know, like Jonson's "Speake that I may see thee," sometimes a blunt command like that reminds us of an act worth remembering because of what it says we wanted to let the world know, do for the world, for ourselves, reveal in a form which, at the time, we didn't realize was the only form. I am a Jew. I am a faithless, sinfully selfish Jew. No. Not that. I am also kind and tender. And enraged and bitter. No. Loving. Not that. Withdrawn and frightened. Generous and wild. Obscene. Heroic, no definitely not that. Innocent, saintly and meek. I am a Jew, and on one particular Halloween thirty years ago I decided to wear a Hitler costume, make it myself. I picked out my wife's gray wool mini-skirt, an old olive drab Army jacket, white button-down Brooks shirt, black tie and rubber boots, and mascaraed that famous stub of a moustache on my upper lip, pasted my hair across forehead and showed up at the party we were invited to. The thing to consider is the feeling, how I felt that night living behind the identity of a stranger, how true to him I was, how true to myself, why I chose to be him. Or not. No. Not that. I am a Jew. I wore that costume as a Jew, I wanted to mirror his murderous depraved self, the faggot Nazi coward behind the mobs and slaughters. And yet at times I've heard that selfsame twittering fairy's voice in my own head, an imitation of an imitation, heterosexual me imitating the finicky artificiality of the queen. Sometimes I hear it at the mirror, shaving, backed with anger, as other voices have behind them a feeling, an as-yet-unidentified emotion connected to no one, made less dangerous that way, so the voice, always an unknown voice, is a mask for the feeling, for something we believe is terrible about ourselves: as if behind who we are – "identity" is our favorite word for it – as if back "there" an infinite self actually is everyone in pure possibility and identity – that skin or image I call Steve – as if who we are isn't much more than a social grace, a bow to the necessity of getting along in life. As if, after all, the "I" is pure interpretation. But not that either. Not that. Not anything I understand. Unless this fantasy explains it – at the party I enjoyed wearing a skirt, having my cock and balls swing free in no underpants above the open airy hem of the skirt. Is that how women feel? I mean is there a special, brutal hint of freedom and power in having one's crotch so easily entered by the world, so vulnerable to touch? I know how good it is when a woman you love slips her hand into your pocket and hunts for your dick. I remember a girl in New York who never wore underpants so whenever I was with her, or whenever she crossed my mind it was impossible not to see her dark thing bearded and moist laid over the world. I wish I could explain what it was to mimic that faggot asshole. Did he dress up, too, at his coke-high private parties, mincing in front of his officers ad girlfriends, flipping up his skirt, in full red lipstick and rouge, mooning his captive audience whenever its interest waned, ordering his fearful worshippers to find an accurate name for him, his right, real name, and as each one called out his guess, screaming like an infant back at them, "NO. NOT THAT! NOT THAT!"

Lightbulb

It sits on top of an old shadeless gooseneck in his tailorshop
window, a lone light showing nothing, a beacon leading no one
anywhere. Maybe he put it there to ward off thieves, maybe to
remind himself of what he was when he bent over pants and
jackets, sewing the torn cloth. I was walking home up the long
gentle 20th Street hill to my house on Mt. Vernon when I saw
it – the smudged bleak useless window, utterly bare, the bulb
atop the jointed metal stem, no more than 60 watts, like an eye
whose only function is not to see itself, a symbol of the absence
of necessity, a mundane star. I stopped for a minute, stood in
the evening street wondering what it could mean being there
like and unlike anything else, and realized I'd need to know the
man it belonged to. I've seen him taking a walk some days, car-
rying an old cane, in his eighties, up 20th, obviously going
nowhere, blank eyes focused on a distance with nothing in it.
I've seen him sitting in his window above the vacant first floor
shop where the bulb is, a wall of bookcases behind him, watch-
ing TV, the weak blue amoeba-like glare of the screen squirm-
ing over his face. The bulb is merely itself, but tonight it came
to mean something unattainable, impossible to name, like who
and why we are ... "When I was born, fifty-six years ago" ...
would those words lead me to express ... the question, the
sketch of a question? Over the years he's gotten fatter, slowed,
walks more bent over, looks down at the pavement, leaning on
his cane. But no amount of scouring detail will do, no imag-
inary story of a life will make life clearer. Each night the bulb's
on, a dull yellow sphere crowning a skinny spine, an armature
with no sculptor to clothe its being, a glowing shrunken skull.
In a tiny brown photograph, torn off across the bottom, un-
earthed by my daughter from a crumbling book, my mother at
thirteen (high black shiny bangs cut straight across) sits hugging
a white puppy on the front steps of her family's Philadelphia
working class rowhouse. Summer. Mouth open, the puppy

wags its tongue. It stands in her lap. I'd even say it smiles. My mother smiles too, pulling it affectionately against her: its white coat and her white dress merge. "Even when you are touched by the tip of a toenail thoughts of desire arise." White dog, white dress. Sun polishes the gray wooden steps she sits on, the porch behind her head, a row of spindles. Her cheek against the dog's cheek, the bulb glowing all night in the window, are the immortal past, filled with dessicated yearning, with so much absent desire.

HOMAGE TO THE AFTERLIFE

*que el hombre se queda, a veces pensando, como
queriendo llorar . . .*   —VALLEJO

Homage to the Afterlife

Without me, the world became what it was what it always is

Without me, a huge man beat the shit out of me dreaming but was
      beaten across the face and chest head smashed until he died

Without me, cornflowers jack-in-the-pulpits kept flourishing along the
      east wall tucked between rocks

Without me, FBI agents raided artists writers confiscated photos
      manuscripts paintings notes

Without me, the godless mood of a country deepened

Without me, love flickered now and then between one pair of eyes and
      another

Without me, theory blossomed as always pressured by a question

Without me, small groups large groups discussed it but showed up for
      work

Without me, the days the nights the weather seasons varying
      beautifully without hesitation without

Without me, the old answers remained intense humorless intenser died
      out flared up in sleep just they pleased

Without me, whatever gods were proposed spoke were heard faded
      arose were heard

Without me, friends enemies opposites equals understood nothing

Without me, the immense trying broke like waves crying out mercy
      mercy

Without me, who could have spoken any name but his own

Without me, I took your face very very slowly in my hands and kissed
      your eyelids once twice tasted sucked the tip of your nose your
      ears the warm offering of your mouth

Without me, an unsatisfied longing in everyone for understanding
      without words as with the earliest relation to the mother

Without me, the healer said it at all times silence inside without
      needing to know

Without me, dire is the only way one teacher proclaimed dire the basis
      of the dire lesson

Without me, it was I pray to everything from a great book that I

remembered above all the battles of the soul he depicted those
    nights when I'd lie awake my hands a triangle on my chest
    chanting Now I lay me down to sleep

Without me, the big green field the brook beyond the screened porch
    thinking about you your face drained my heart of all the fear
    hatred that ebbs and drowns

Without me, sitting there with you your face the only peaceful silence
    I have ever known one thinks that way without realizing how to
    use it overall

Without me, how you use it in the hours days and years to come is
    what matters how did I

Without me, sunlight changed the green into greens

Without me, a moment or two of nobody in particular

Without me, grammar beautiful virgin of sense got itself fucked by an
    ignorant Jewish escaped slave who questioned her appearance
    her inviolable innocence

Without me, who could have known without me

Without me, stomach cancer heart attack flowers seen the right way

Without me, one's own death linguistically misconceived like calling
    yourself you like using your own name

Without me, time now to admit the real story behind this form this
    refusal this inability to begin otherwise this decision to plead

Without me, the truth is who is left after process has been lived

Without me, now no reason not to

Without me, like a final useless prayer whose aim is always changing
    always within reach always free and kind always open to the
    undying particles of nobody's soul

Without me, noun and pronoun surrender the vast solid gift of
    tangible qualities to the trivial airy link of the lost preposition

Without me, absolutely is the story I confess is here not being hidden
    really is the story about a great love affair

Without me, fits of vomiting and the duty of saying no if there is a
    god then that's the heresy

Without me, I had this idea for a game three days long two people
    play no sleep until it's over one question is asked back and forth
    once each turn by each player Do you believe in God? and the
    other is only allowed to laugh back and forth each time for three
    days but the laughs have to convey something meaningful like a

real answer the laughs have to be expressive like facial gestures
are

Without me, the sacred objects left behind by the dead faded back to
the ordinary the unpossessable the miraculous transience the
cosmic perceptual contract behind us and it

Without me, my old mom's beak of a nose in profile socked into the
universe by the morphine drip caught the early morning sun
through the hospital window a faint thin golden line along the
nosebone like a blade or a wing never again forever I could hear
defining the silence between us

Without me, how real we appear to each other even playing tennis
naked out back like the Blakes then a drink naked then my you-
know-what in your you-know-what without pretty description
sorry balls rackets strewn on the court twilight glazing our fair
bodies purple

Without me, back to the wetness theme

Without me, I could try philosophy but it would kill hard-ons wanting
your funny puss as long as I have a face you have a place to sit a
Southern gent next to me at the airport bar whispered watching
the waitress bend over to pick up a napkin

Without me, a word is like a note struck on a keyboard said the
famous pioneer in innocent philosophizing

Without me, one instruction for reading this is jump or stop or don't
care while you skim

Without me, ignorance flew its blind kite into the realm where eyes
believe someone is waiting

Without me, don't bother me she said I'm done

Without me, how define immortality how phrase that oh so heavy
question L.W. would sneer and ask what is accomplished by
such a gesture

Without me, who? what? only where when

Without me, blindness, silence, listening until every sound is

Without me, all men

Without me, abstraction lost its appetite for the consoling the real
image the meaty detail to believe in

Without me, you can't describe a feeling of course you can think about
particular cases scenes rooms words

Without me, how does hoping someone will return express itself there

are no hope movements are there no wing-like icons manifesting
     our final future
Without me, like this like that disappear
Without me, envy conquers envy
Without me, the whole secret lies in arbitrariness according to S.K.
Without me, the Socratic vanishing moment teaches all now
Without me, Mary Lee who lived up at the old house made coffee a
     glass broke off in my mouth peanut butter probably I
     swallowed glass Mary Lee shook me I was two-and-a-half and
     after that she always threatened us she'd go to New York it was
     our fault her martyrdom and this is the little story my wife
     came up with they had no idea what children were about she
     added wounds headaches she had headaches trauma dreams
Without me, the true story gets told
Without me, several days' memories ooze into the dream
Without me, what was that
Without me, access to another degree of meaning paid heavily hearing
     the shadow mouth
Without me, crippled refrain of absent humanity singing itself to sleep
     now down to sleep
Without me, my dream My name is Louise I love you Steve in a sweet
     wee child voice face looking up at me held in my arms on the
     empty dance floor I never could dance but I kiss her face like a
     mother
Without me, everyone knows everything no middle as the great one
     said at the end of an early work
Without me, death is not an event in life we do not live to experience
     death
Without me, philosophy finally *is* philosophy motes in an ever-
     changing light
Without me, let's say you're looking in a mirror just to see how you
     look nothing more a flower seeing a flower
Without me, the syllogism of desire equally two unaccountably gets
     carved on all the altars
Without me, worship is seen for what it is self-condemnation
Without me, and I and you forever phrases out of a book found in a
     burnt-up house establish the age of the eye-level god

Without me, no surrealism no 18th century couplets no enjambment
no acephalic foot none of that prosodic yesterday and tomorrow
no elision and yet this beauty haunts the hand that loves them
like one woman's face loved more than anything guides the
living hand abandons the living hand on the dark margin
Without me, a surprising inner trembling no name in the midst of so
much clever wording revision forced excellence the terrible need
the wait someone behind someone behind someone
Without me, the uselessness of trying
Without me, so much not understanding even Henry James bewildered
wiped out by without me
Without me, all's lost and yet and yet
Without me, the approximation of what is to the ideal nagging at us
minute after minute like a bad tooth is the perfect hinge on
which the door to the real swings open
Without me, insight wisdom those wonderful near-twins dance in the
moonlight their tiny genitals glowing letting us know exactly
where they are and what movements occur should we join them
Without me, all the masters
Without me, all the masters pose the selfsame question I mean answer
to the student I mean master
Without me, the story of the Not Two doesn't need words to be
known or
Without me, whose forgotten kisses they were faded forever I hoped
on my lips but only on mine
Without me, love rose through veins and muscles until skin became
sky
Without me, every professing Christian became the host every Jew the
guest
Without me, Whitman's self did in fact commit its very existence to
the space beneath your bootsole
Without me, Yeats spoke as himself for the first time sounded like
Yeats
Without me, and now the true the real story begins and begins
Without me, with me all else awake
Without me, sitting breathing I fell asleep dreaming of a knish woke
built a temple nobody allowed in or out

Without me, there is no you to say I

Without me, words are like the film on deep water like breath on a
    cold window

Without me, you I

Without me, syntax is the order of the mind as it is as it is not before
    after silence speech like a hand plunged into boiling water
    waving goodbye

Without me, how crucial it is to see happy no matter what or it all
    collapses

Without me, speaking silently inner speaking I have come to believe is
    the

Without me, don't watch what you do can't watch watch touch this
    thing what is it

Without me, whatever we see is losing its balance rain flooding the
    clear shallow creek flooding the pond the noise of its pouring
    out invisible

Without me, dreams flower in the air too quick to see

Without me, ask

Without me, the arbitrary in oneself corresponds to the accidental in
    the world

Without me, nothing is possible but the bare name

Without me, forget the sadness of having been

Without me, always the other only the other

Without me, gratitude for a chair for a bed gratitude even for weeping
    at a table

Without me, each thing cup hat shoes fork knife gives itself is

Without me, lawless wingèd unconfined and breaks all chains from
    every mind Blake calls love

Without me, the blue sea produces yellow dust

Without me, the waves of the ocean of pain are very deep how can we
    make a raft to cross it with wood

Without me, we are living time

Without me, the time of speaking measures the soul and the quality of
    that soul speaking

Without me, if God looked into our minds could he see who we are
    speaking of

Without me, words look at me hear me

Without me, a cry tortures itself with thoughts

Without me, the whole point emerges

Without me, how can there be a story a past an I did this and that
history the importance of having been

Without me, who cares whose name is carried on the granite
grassmarker Oh that's Jack remember him No

Without me, no concepts of meaning

Without me, the description of the use of a word is the description of
a system or systems

Without me, using without me to forget the story

Without me, what makes sense a fly meandering along the top of this
page waking in the dark to the guilt the done undone frog adrift
on its back like a sleeping baby

Without me, the rocks don't move the stream flows over them

Without me, dreams of friends' faces awake asleep the daily I
submerged they continue forever

Without me, the sky's a house for everyone of course not

Without me, no matter how stupid this obsession it's the scream Rilke
said and it screams for you

Without me, heathen eyes reading treat each word like a threat a
desperate attempt to find at least one believable religious truth

Without me, a little gentle touch under the sheets before falling asleep
two feet ankles thighs the comfort of loose hands warmth of
another

Without me, and the darkness the endless light of without me already
letting itself be known to the cells to the waking mind the
practice the griefless disappearance

Without me, no question about the suffering always there somewhere
to give speech the urgent nudge it needs the pang of its
unrewarded crawl across

Without me, fear the practice love the practice vanishing practice the
slow vanishing leaf to trunk of the trees

Without me, no not fear nothing but fear

Without me, one face on the pillow her last face silence her shrinking
into the brass box of ashen lumps the practice rattle

Without me, beyond

Without me, singed by the suffering twilight pale red hills the cloudy

residues grass minnows the shimmering pond fleet fish
Without me, stuttering established as the new international language of
    feeling
Without me, no mere accident hesitant unsure I can't yet lift myself
    above the mass of appearances
Without me, the story goes like this I was
Without me, the story the real story that is begins when Joan gets up
    on a beautiful sunny morning finds her car stolen no she's back
    in the car again with
Without me, did God make heaven and earth they were not they were
    they were not
Without me, still the old jail dreams haunt rant still not availing their
    necessary lesson
Without me, dream of the right hand fingers lopped off and the left
    thumb still not fathomed
Without me, the essential guilt of having been the unconscious story
    before life after
Without me, Because you exist he answered when I asked him Why
    did my mother hate me so much Because you exist
Without me, on the other hand the word God
Without me, the story the search for its mortal meaning goes on
    among the lines the absent one I was you you were in this
    reverie of one's own absence forever I will be will be forever
    not here not there in nobody's mind practice
Without me, how can we face it and love how can it be
Without me, the story has to be its own teller now that the speaker is
    dead
Without me, the agony threads through it all which is love loss grief
    and the death of it all awareness of that at some level always
    without me above all gratitude the lesson
Without me, heart as if you never spoke never got to say how only
    the moments of feeling matter the ephemeral myths of truth
    mean all the rest detail sad uninspired waiting for the emotional
    story for the touch of truth
Without me, someday when I lose you will you still be able to sleep
Without me, ashamed of your ignorance helplessness to speak of what
    we do not understand is the story
Without me, I saw it and find not one word that can

Without me, slave to the universe the universe voiceless wonder
Without me, objectivity's fascination heralded a laugh an abject idea
Without me, subjectivity's inescapable glamour mounted a fresh horse
Without me, evaporation of the huge cosmic twins was what replaced
     my poor moth-like life which not even memory a few years
     later sustained conveyed a few shards white laughter
Without me, everyone fantasizes himself a lost twin
Without me, at death the other one is born found
Without me, who cared about wife daughters books house flowers
     pants bowls the facts
Without me, what were the generations but a chain finally ending at
     its last link the edge where we are
Without me, now perhaps that link that edge is like a night space there
     not there we here you and it unendingly welded into a single
     point voiceless open gone into it still standing here
Without me, where you are sings one tiny harrowing note of love no
     one to listen no one to touch that single what was it
Without me, heart space where nothing is possessed and therefore
     according to the one true law of love love simply is because it
     needs itself above all as a proof of God
Without me, the idea of it the belief in it the knowledge of it sunset's
     bawdy pinks and grays strewn across the grassy layers of heaven
     wet grass the ragged blackening trees crickets
Without me, whosoever shall lose his life shall find it but how when
     are you sure what bullshit
Without me, *that it exists* who can experience the duration of ignorance
     necessary to know *that it exists* mystical primitive glimpse of a
     grateful god
Without me, the story of the song that put me to sleep lullaby
     together without me down to sleep now I lay me
Without me, everything found its true perspective ease of the weather
     surrender of the ash
Without me, I returned and lived again believe me exactly as before
     same man same life every detail at every moment in every place
     exactly the same except this time suffused by the quiet joy of
     acceptance what a phrase by the joyless quiet of with
     unacceptable perfection
Without me, all the worshipped names were subtracted to leave the

real story clear stripped bare intact legible ours fierce like the
 ocean
Without me, but the greatest of these charity felt lived nevertheless on
 other hand but well maybe what about
Without me, beareth all things etc however
Without me, that last argument on the bus about tomatoes and the
 way she told me to lower my voice in the restaurant however
Without me, eyes upon eyes and the feelings in the eyes
 interpenetrating souls became flesh that dreg of unreachable
 inner
Without me, who could know who could have been
Without me, who could have imagined the place gratitude filled at the
 center of it hatred's foil
Without me, the odor of the field rising a bread-smell above the pond
 mist tales and stories are the outer garment but we are bound to
 penetrate beyond
Without me, it's the stories and the beyond that become the single
 blossom of the universe he held up those hated generalities no
 mortal can exceed or express or approach Hegel maybe though
 always that's where we want ourselves are then dinner's on this
 life is so
Without me, what was blood and darkness in an animal grew on in us
 to soul and continues to scream out as soul and it screams for
 you you mouth you sayer of us God Rilke was such a
Without me, not knowing who speaks and hears and pauses syllable
 by syllable language cannot complete itself or the one who uses
 it
Without me, that's the story and the heart the delicate core distant up
 against us like the air itself in us
Without me, nothing persuades us everything persuades us
Without me, let me tell you about when she first found out she had
 stomach cancer before the operation a few days before she
 turned to me it was at night like a small beast glaring at its prey
 and screamed at her only child mind you me in fact My life is
 over and so is yours
Without me, who does not think of himself is given the keys
Without me, if I could give you the heart of my heart could let you

know I know it as you do times when the eyes and heart felt
like one surging blaze of

Without me, the doctor answers my pleading question Why did she
hate me so much with Because you exist

Without me, but that is not the story it's beyond not in details
memories feelings washed up into the present by the wounds
struggles to understand to survive walk talk eat work sleep and
in between the story

Without me, wanting to understand wanting to get rid of who we are
what's happened to us and not act can't have accept can't accept

Without me, there is no understanding intellect is absorbed by the fact
of not being here of having been of the infinite final loss which
is our suffering before it occurs

Without me, listen to the nonexistent text silence beyond the audible
absence of any sound word the sleep voice Breton's shadow
mouth Longinus's speaker's risk that more earthly rhetorical
term

Without me, as if you need not listen are listening listening to itself
without me beyond what you can say are being heard really yes
I'm listening the air was listening to us on the quiet twilit porch
who were we

Without me, I wanted this to I have to confess help I mean possibly
console in some way but halfway through I knew it was wrong
knew it couldn't too many motives too much blind greed
stupidity the needs hungers moral violence of having a self
unable to give beyond its who knows beyond its need to be rid
of itself

Without me, continuous transition . . . the strategic point at which if a
hole be made all the corruptions of dialectics and all the
metaphysical fictions pour into our philosophy

Without me, believe in the guesses of your teachers

Without me, beyond the daily ruse of narrative detail that feeds the
story-hunger the need for meaning based on our gift of
perceptual continuity meaning built on what happened instead of
on awe as if we always need a cure before going forth into

Without me, scenes that won't fade won't pass into the light traces
memories of faces ideas about God a life after hurt voices that

tried to make lovesongs that would turn heaven into earth
Without me, once when and believe me it's so difficult to get this
straight so important these paradigms of the day's daily ruse
mask that is everything paradigms of the broken heart torn to
pieces embodiments of profound loss or not having been given
what one needs that only the idea of God suffices sorry the story
but which one first the subjective (for those who live in the
present) – which is always about doubt – a time when I well
there was this girl from a distance I could barely see her face
how she looked I never did love I mean never could love I never
have known what love is she was standing in the schoolyard
when I first saw her blond curls little blue dress really such love
I guess poured out such ridiculously fraught longing for what
I've only just 45 years later begun to realize I still can't quite
grasp what it is what need flared but the particular scene I
remember now best involves He jests at scars that never felt a
wound buried second line of that great soliloquy who was she
anyway a vanishing of air certainly now no more than that god
what a rending to have been there at all what an impossible
thing we are the scene is like a headache coming on one has to
deal with it somehow the grief of a love the silent needy mirrors
we are like mouths where we were broken off from the other
that's what this is really about untranscendent ramblings that
occur at that spot the mirror-mouth but I have to tell this one
by now I'm not sure which girl it was exactly but the scene's
the same almost first heaven the expanse of space that seems to
be over the earth like a dome the dwelling place of the Deity
and the joyful abode of the blessed dead a spiritual state of
everlasting communion with God a place or condition of utmost
happiness preceded in the dictionary by heave an upward
motion a rhythmical rising And while it worked it made me
think Of timber's varied doom One inch where people eat and
drink The next inch in a tomb or That high compassion which
can overbear Reluctance for pure loving-kindness' sake the
scene's we were sitting in a car hers because I didn't have one
talking looking out over the fields into a small dark wood you
could hear the trees their blackness their massive black blue

spoke in that tongue to be ours while we tried to touch without
seeming to want to tongue soon to be ours but when I let my
right arm slip down on the seat behind you I felt your hair
rested it on your shoulder actually made my fingers explore
now and then register textures of skin and hair and underneath
flesh the bones that seem so far from the exterior beauty of
appearance then hand and arm fully pressed against you from
behind I don't remember tenderness more like euphoric fear or
any of the so-called higher feelings just the wanting throb in my
neck and face and groin my whole face was like a hand opening
to receive a gift feeling it enter the palm did you ever see a bird
land suddenly on a bare branch brake halt in air clutch then look
around with that quick twitching littleness all of itself so brief
delicate unknowing that you and it you watching it almost made
you impossible to yourself should I be here or are we made
much more possible full of simply our own forgotten presence
absorbed I shift closer on the seat against her the least pulses of
my body shake but look at Rimbaud the gunrunner and the
shambles of his desire winding up a Catholic writing to his
sister in 1891 June with that leg of his now a contemporary
myth of lost love listen to Rimbaud in a letter to his sister, "The
stockings are useless. I will sell them somewhere." why do I feel
that encapsulates the terrorist war-hungry genosuicidal twentieth
century's sick heart without me without me without me without
me without me I moved my shoulder against hers she leaned her
head against mine would this cure the night summer my face
hers apprehending something in them beyond them physical
mouths opening "My life is over and so is yours" transcendent
paranoid ma whorled souls tongues reaping each other where
the Who am I is answered in the other's absolute giving to you
its who which isn't a question anyway I think I started thinking
then then stopped listening to the stars enter the human faint
indeterminate breaths exhaled space matroclinous longings a
calm an infant's sense its mother listens with the understanding
of a proximate god that needs nothing for the moment but her
listening our faces dying to enter each other to redeem the as yet
unknown knowledge of not understanding the irremediables

fumbling buttons this is not possible one by one slipping a
button through its hole unzipping my fly whose hands was it
hers or mine no loneliness and as I write Burney's WW II
loneliness in 18 months of solitary I found that the muscles of
my mouth he says had become stiff and unwilling and that the
thoughts and questions I had wanted to express became
ridiculous when I turned them into words Solitude had so far
weaned me from the habit of intercourse, even the intercourse
of speculation, that I could no longer see any relationship with
another person unless it were introduced gradually by a long
overture of common trivialities Once when I was allowed to
exercise outside (and that was very rare) I brought to my cell a
snail It was company of a sort and as it were an emissary from
the world of real life hearing the *attitude* in her voice I wonder if
that's possible so no matter what she says even silence the tone
might be unadulterated hatred the song of the soul heard
through the mask of appearances last instant of the future
glimmering on her snail-tongue mother as she withdraws its tip
from between her lips and slowly closes her mouth into a blank
slit do we see everything through desire the dooming lens shield
of desire held up against the other's career of maintaining a self
Because you exist those three words or My life is over and so is
yours mother to son both deaths instigating the birth of the
afterlife for when do we ever discover it except in the abrupt
murderousness of one's own terror reaching beyond to the one
closest to us though even she can't help which redoubles the
terror this suicidal edge of love is the edge of self where
appearances yield bestial heaven O my regrets my stupidity but
in the car it was otherwise there was this there was this
unimaginable unpredictable my sweet this for we are imagined
ones you imagined by me and I by you after life how can we
discover it in the car moonlight splashed it was otherwise before
I knew it she stripped open her cotton dress tearing at buttons
down the front wanting me to see I want you to see it she said
Death may come in many forms they say but truly it comes in
only one which is the end of love (Carruth) wanting me to see
her near-naked undiscovered self I want someone to discover me

a friend told me his wife screamed at him near the end of their divorce to be discovered don't we wish what could possibly make a difference to our final knowledge *this is I am* two phrases as close to descriptions of god as we'll get with the exception of concrete mystical-vision images horses with flaming tongues the yielding to these the homage the enslavement reverent feudal disciple to an undiscovered Lord I want someone to discover me well I was discovered believe me when my mother raged out of her mind and spat My life is over and so is yours at the top of her lungs by the sea four days before they opened her to be discovered I found out is to be established as someone who listens as an anonymous space her nipples in the car under the streetlamp raised through the sheer bra cloth large firm her panties a wispy path of hair running above the top to the rim of the navel I could see it her skin a kind of holy whiteness glowing in the car eyes closed her hand soothing it like something very precious kissing the head necessary strong beloved by which a man knows in which world he lives and by which death is hollowed into a mere fable a harmless ghost floating in the mind for a while especially when a woman we love touches going back now I begin to realize after all these years a few things important I hope in my blindness after the false life brief in semiconscious sleep people who are going to be important to us we meet not just once but at least twenty times before we begin to take the signs and we avoid them as long as we possibly can because the grief of a love to redeem oneself as oneself and others as they are shatters the who finally forever

My life is over and so is yours let's agree she had no choice she had to say it it was her only authentic release the truth of who she was about her state when she was told about the cancer and then was forced to face without really being aware of it her hellish dependence on me so I listened to it let it in if I did not exist would she have been happier yes almost surely yes then what a different life o conscience fear
Without me, asking the shrink Why did she hate me so much and hearing Because you exist

Without me, she the world my world would not have been an obstacle
        another consciousness to feed tend worry about know accept
        Because you exist
Without me, the index of the soul would have shifted like weather
        from deep vermilion gray to greenish gold Because you exist
Without me, the archaeology of pain would have begun in another not
        me Because you exist
Without me, no hiding no constant urge to escape timid little creature
        lunging into the brush Because you exist
Without me, in the car all we did was touch each other everywhere
        even vagina and breasts thick delicate wet hair even her
        shadowy eyes held me in a trance of meaning My life is over
        and so is yours not there then in the car suddenly opening her
        dress herself because of my fear at the time later it would appear
        as car wrecks drugs lack of compassion refusal to work gestures
        of veiled hatred suicidal glee metaphorical embodiments and yet
        at the core was the desire to love reaching out not the analytical
        hesitation on the threshold of experience the rehearsal by
        thought but the simple honest urge to embrace Because you
        exist
Without me, so I found myself doing just that embracing her in her
        dire illness her terror of the end I don't think she could ask why
        she was as she was or perhaps she did but it changed nothing
        People don't change she used to say or reveal the doubting core
        torturing her minutes I found myself over the next two years
        taking care of the same woman who hated me with such
        uncensored fury Because you exist that god-like response
        beyond the personal daily recognitions of identity we share to
        keep ourselves sane to hold ourselves together irrefutably royal
        in a weird impersonal tone that defined my existence from the
        beginning once for all how could that wound be healed how can
        you tell me except through love which is still impossible except
        at rare times of . . . we enter the world so helplessly must witness
        each other's helplessness in order to love . . . one particular night
        in the hospital I remember we both acknowledged how close
        her death was how soon it would be she could barely form
        words find words because of the morphine and I found myself

holding her stroking her hair smoothing her entire face with my
face and hands repeatedly leaning over her drained body skeletal
waif with all of myself trying to cradle her bring her into me as
if she might live a waif inside my body waif if only I could
contain her leaving her upper arms like wrists all the flesh eaten
inward by the thing inside all our deaths presented in her death
Because you exist waif

Without me, they decided to administer the morphine drip the week
before her doctor had said Hilda, we're old friends and the news
drove her wild they had to put her in restraints wild waif even
that feeble dread she had become in restraints now under the
drip she was calm head propped up against three pillows
counterpane folded a few inches beneath her neck hair combed
waif with that miniature barrette she always wore to pull the
hair back over her ear arms down by her sides but she could
hear what I whispered "I should have been kinder to you" and
raised her right hand tapped herself on the shoulder

Without me, I'm standing on a dance floor alone apparently but I feel
a gentle hand resting on my shoulder as if an invisible partner
stood facing me I look down I'm cradling a tiny sweet-faced
baby in my arms she opens her eyes and looks up at me and for
a split second I realize then forget it's in a dream she looks up at
me and nearly sings in a tiny voice "My name is Louise, I love
you, Steve" I bend my head to her and kiss her and wake not in
tears really use resurrected from explanation to explanation freed
from one mind to another we go resurrected

Without me, she couldn't use the potty by the bed Did the doctor tell
you anything Did he tell *you* anything I asked her back instead
of an answer It's back in the lungs Yes I know I let myself say
then and her eyes opened a little seeking me or she just wanted
them open when she said "Well, that's the end of my story"

Stephen Berg's poems, versions and translations have been published widely. He was awarded Guggenheim, National Endowment for the Arts, Pennsylvania Council, Rockefeller, and Dietrich Foundation fellowships, as well as *Poetry* magazine's Frank O'Hara Memorial Prize. Currently professor of English at the University of the Arts, he has taught at Haverford and Princeton, and founded and co-edits the *American Poetry Review*. With painter Tom Chimes, he was commissioned by the Fairmount Park Art Association to create the public art project *Sleeping Woman,* installed in 1991 along Philadelphia's Kelly Drive on the edge of the Schuylkill River.